Lectionary Worship Aids

Series IX, Cycle C

for the Revised Common Lectionary

by George Reed, O.S.L.

An Anthology of Worship Resources from
The Immediate Word
a Component of SermonSuite.com
from CSS Publishing Company

CSS Publishing Company, Inc.
Lima, Ohio

FIRST EDITION
Copyright © 2012
by CSS Publishing Co., Inc.

For more information about CSS Publishing Company resources, visit our website at www.csspub.com or email us at csr@csspub.com or call (800) 241-4056.

ISBN-13: 978-0-7880-2674-4
ISBN-10: 0-7880-2674-7

PRINTED IN USA

To my wife, Betty,
whose constant love and support has been my greatest joy.

Table of Contents

Easter Season

Season of Pentecost

Music Resources

UMH: United Methodist Hymnal
H82: The Hymnal 1982 (The Episcopal Church)
LBW: Lutheran Book of Worship
PH: Presbyterian Hymnal
CH: Chalice Hymnal
NCH: The New Century Hymnal
NNBH: The New National Baptist Hymnal
AAHH: African-American Heritage Hymnal
CCB: Cokesbury Chorus Book
RENEW: Renew! Songs & Hymns for Blended Worship
ELA: Evangelical Lutheran Worship

Introduction

Early in the history of CSS Publishing Company, we realized that there was a need to provide fresh and relevant worship resources to our customers. Over the years, many different volumes have been developed as an answer to that need. These resources include numerous volumes of *Lectionary Worship Aids*, the *Lectionary Worship Workbook*, and many others.

We live in a world that seems to move faster all the time. Our society continues to react more quickly to the events that go on around us. CSS Publishing has continued to try to fill the need to help pastors relate those current events in their preaching and teaching, so CSS created a unique service called **The Immediate Word**, an integral part of *SermonSuite.com*, to assist pastors in tying important news items to God's word. *SermonSuite.com* is a compilation of preaching and worship material that is presented for timely use each week for the parish pastor. The **TIW** team of practicing parish clergy examines current events each week and seeks God's guidance in connecting the assigned lectionary readings with news and current events happening in the world every day. Even though the worship resources were written for a specific time with **TIW**, the writing is relevant for any and every day.

Included in **The Immediate Word** is a worship resource that helps the parish pastor plan for weekly worship. As with previous volumes in this series, this collection contains resources such as calls to worship, hymn selections, and prayers that relate to the lectionary for each week.

This volume contains a collection of these resources for Cycle C of the Revised Common Lectionary that has been gleaned from **The Immediate Word**. It is our prayer that this resource will prove to be an invaluable asset to the success of your ministry.

The editors of CSS Publishing Company, Inc.

Advent 1

Jeremiah 33:14-16
1 Thessalonians 3:9-13
Luke 21:25-36

Call to Worship
Leader: To God we lift up our souls.
People: It is in God that we trust.
Leader: Help us to know your ways, O God.
People: Teach us your paths.
Leader: All the paths of God are steadfast love and faithfulness
People: for those who keep God's covenant and decrees.

OR

Leader: Come, let us worship the God who comes to us.
People: We come with thanksgiving and awe.
Leader: We worship the God who created us all.
People: We worship the God who became one of us.
Leader: We anticipate God's coming in fullness.
People: We celebrate God's glorious future for us.

Hymns and Sacred Songs
"I Want to Be Ready"
found in:
UMH: 722   NCH: 616

"My Lord, What a Morning"
found in:
UMH: 719   NNBH: 499
PH: 449   CH: 708
AAHH: 195

"O Come, O Come Emmanuel"
found in:
UMH: 211
H82: 56
PH: 9
AAHH: 188
NNBH: 82
NCH: 116
CH: 119
LBW: 34

"Lift Up Your Heads, Ye Mighty Gates"
found in:
UMH: 213
H82: 436
PH: 8
NCH: 117
CH: 129
LBW: 32

"This Is a Day of New Beginnings"
found in:
UMH: 383
NCH: 417
CH: 518

"Let There Be Peace on Earth"
found in:
UMH: 431
NCH: 677

"Rejoice, the Lord Is King"
found in:
UMH: 715/716
H82: 481
PH: 155
NCH: 303
CH: 699
LBW: 171

Prayer for the Day / Collect

O God, who holds us and the future in your hands, grant us the faith to trust that your steadfast love and faithfulness will bring us to glory with all your creation; through Jesus Christ our Savior. Amen.

OR

We come into your presence, O God, to offer our praise and thanksgiving for all that you have done for us and for all that you have in store for us. Fill us with your love and grace that we may anticipate with joy the glory that is about to be revealed. Amen.

Prayer of Confession

Leader: Let us confess to God and before one another our sins and especially the ways that we place our desires on God.

People: We confess to you, O God, and before one another that we have sinned. We have not made idols with our hands, but we have made them with our minds. We have taken our own thoughts and desires and molded a god that looks like us. We have taken the scriptures you have given for our enlightenment and salvation and turned them into a reflection of the way we want things to be. All of this comes from our failure to come to know you better. Forgive us and turn us from our idols to a true and deep relationship with you. Open our hearts and our minds that we may truly be your people. Amen.

Leader: God is in the business of salvation, the salvation of all us sinners. Know that God loves you and forgives you and desires nothing more than to be in a loving relationship with you, revealing the divine self to us as God already knows us.

Prayers of the People (and the Lord's Prayer)

We worship and adore you, O God, because you are not like us. You are beyond us in power and majesty and you are beyond us in love and service. Our words of description for you are weak and pathetic compared to the reality they seek to describe.

(The following paragraph may be used if a separate prayer of confession has not been used.)

We confess to you, O God, and before one another that we have sinned. We have not made idols with our hands, but we have made them with our minds. We have taken our own thoughts and desires and molded a god that looks like us. We have taken the scriptures you have given for our enlightenment and salvation and turned them into a reflection of the way we want things to be. All of this comes from our failure to know you better. Forgive us and turn us from our idols to a true and deep relationship with you. Open our hearts and our minds that we may truly be your people.

We give you thanks for the salvation you bring to us each day. You come and bring love and grace to us when we least expect it. You shower your creation with love and tenderness in spite of our sinfulness.

(Other thanksgivings may be offered.)

We pray for one another in our need and for all who long with you for the fullness of your salvation. As you move among us and bring your healing Spirit to us, empower us to work with you, being your physical presence for those in need.

(Other intercessions may be offered.)

All these things we ask in the name of our Savior Jesus Christ, who taught us to pray together, saying:
Our Father... Amen.

(Or if the Lord's Prayer is not used at this point in the service)
All this we ask in the name of the Blessed and Holy Trinity. Amen.

Advent 2

Malachi 3:1-4
Philippians 1:3-11
Luke 3:1-6

Call to Worship
Leader: Blessed be the God of Israel,
People: who has looked favorably on us and redeemed us.
Leader: God has raised up a mighty Savior for us in the house of David,
People: just as spoken through the mouth of the holy prophets from of old,
Leader: God said that we would be saved from our enemies
People: and from the hand of all who hate us.

OR

Leader: Come and see the salvation of our God!
People: We long for God's saving work among us!
Leader: God will fill the valleys and level the high places.
People: God will straighten out even crooked ways.
Leader: God's work will begin in us!
People: Yes, God! Come and place us on the straight and narrow way to salvation!

Hymns and Sacred Songs
"Hail to the Lord's Anointed"
found in:
UMH: 203   CH: 140
H82: 616   LBW: 87
AAHH: 187   ELW: 311
NCH: 104   Renew: 101

"O Come, O Come, Emmanuel"
found in:

UMH: 211	NCH: 116
H82: 56	CH: 119
PH: 9	LBW: 34
AAHH: 188	ELW: 257
NNBH: 82	

"I Want to Walk As a Child of the Light"
found in:

UMH: 206	ELW: 815
H82: 490	Renew: 152

"Blessed Be the God of Israel"
found in:

UMH: 209	ELW: 250/552
H82: 444	Renew: 128
CH: 135	

"Lift Up Your Heads, Ye Mighty Gates"
found in:

UMH: 213	CH: 129
H82: 436	LBW: 32
PH: 8	Renew: 59
NCH: 117	

"Savior of the Nations, Come"
found in:

UMH: 214	LBW: 28
PH: 14	ELW: 263

"This Is a Day of New Beginnings"
found in:

UMH: 383	CH: 518
NCH: 417	

"O Come and Dwell in Me"
found in:
UMH: 388

"Change My Heart, O God"
found in:
CCB: 56   Renew: 143

"Humble Yourself in the Sight of the Lord"
found in:
CCB: 72   Renew: 188

Prayer for the Day / Collect
O God, who desires to save and redeem all creation, grant us the faith to place ourselves in your hands that we may turn our lives around and walk in your ways; through Jesus Christ our Savior. Amen.

OR

We have come to worship you, O God, and to prepare for your coming among us. Open our hearts and minds that we may turn our lives around in true repentance so that we may walk with Jesus. Amen.

Prayer of Confession
Leader: Let us confess to God and before one another our sins and especially our unwillingness to see ourselves as sinners in need of salvation.
People: We confess to you, O God, and before one another that we have sinned. We want to think of ourselves in only good terms. We hide our faults and sins and thus deny ourselves the opportunity to repent and become more like our Savior, Jesus. Give us the faith in your love

to look at ourselves clearly and admit who we have become. **Forgive us our sinful ways and empower us with your Spirit to turn our lives around and to serve you fully as your redeemed children. Amen.**
Leader: God invites us to confess not so we can be forgiven but so we can be honest with ourselves and with God about who we are. God forgives us and empowers us to be the children of God.

Prayers of the People (and the Lord's Prayer)
We praise your name, O God, as the salvation of all creation. Your loving grace is around and within all that you have made.

(The following paragraph may be used if a separate prayer of confessions has not been used.)
We confess to you, O God, and before one another that we have sinned. We want to think of ourselves in only good terms. We hide our faults and sins and thus deny ourselves the opportunity to repent and become more like our Savior, Jesus. Give us the faith in your love to look at ourselves clearly and admit who we have become. Forgive us our sinful ways and empower us with your Spirit to turn our lives around and to serve you fully as your redeemed children.

We give our thanks for all your blessings and especially for your invitation to be transformed into your image. We thank you for the opportunity to repent and to be made new.

(Other thanksgivings may be offered.)
We pray for one another in our need and we are especially aware of the ways your creation is rushing to destruction, never heeding your call to turn and return to your life. As you continue to call, help us to be your loving presence that echoes your grace.

(Other intercessions may be offered.)
All these things we ask in the name of our Savior Jesus Christ, who taught us to pray together, saying:
Our Father... Amen.

(Or if the Lord's Prayer is not used at this point in the service)
All this we ask in the name of the Blessed and Holy Trinity. Amen.

Advent 3

Zephaniah 3:14-20
Philippians 4:4-7
Luke 3:7-18

Call to Worship
Leader: Surely God is our salvation.
People: We will trust and not be afraid.
Leader: God is our strength and our might.
People: God has become our salvation.
Leader: Shout aloud and sing for you,
People: for great in our midst is the Holy One of Israel.

OR

Leader: God calls us to come and worship.
People: All of us together? Even those we despise?
Leader: All are God's children. All need God's grace.
People: We know they need forgiveness.
Leader: Grace comes to those who themselves need grace.
People: When I'm honest I know I need grace a lot.
Leader: God calls us all to come and worship.
People: I see the viper within as well as without. I come, O God.

Hymns and Sacred Songs
"It's Me, It's Me, O Lord" ("Standing in the Need of Prayer")
found in:
UMH: 352   CH: 579
NNBH: 496

"Help Us to Accept Each Other"
found in:
UMH: 560   NCH: 388
PH: 358   CH: 487

"In Christ There Is No East or West"
found in:
UMH: 548   NNBH: 299
H82: 529   NCH: 394/395
PH: 439/440   CH: 687
AAHH: 398/399   LBW: 259

"Just As I Am"
found in:
UMH: 357   NNBH: 167
H82: 693   NCH: 207
PH: 371   CH: 339
AAHH: 344/345   LBW: 296

"All People that on Earth Do Dwell"
found in:
UMH: 75   NCH: 7
H82: 377/378   CH: 18
PH: 220/221   LBW: 245
NNBH: 36

"Blest Be the Dear Uniting Love"
found in:
UMH: 566

"Something Beautiful"
found in:
CCB: 84

"Sanctuary"
found in:
CCB: 87

Prayer for the Day / Collect
O God, who created us all out of the same dust and filled us
with the same divine breath, grant us the grace to admit that
it is we who stand in the need of prayer, grace, and forgiveness. Amen.

OR

Jesus, you came and were defamed, and yet you opened not
your mouth to defend yourself. As we come into your presence, teach us to examine our lives as easily as we examine
the lives of others. Amen.

Prayer of Confession
Leader: Let us confess to God and before one another our
sins and especially the ways in which we vilify others and
excuse our own failures.
People: **We confess to you, O God, and before one another that we have sinned. We have not lived out of your
Spirit of forgiveness and acceptance but rather have demonized others while overlooking our own sins. We confess that we are sinners. No one this week mistook us for
you. We have much to learn and to become. Forgive us
and empower us with your Spirit that we may truly accept others as we become more and more like our Savior.
Amen.**
Leader: Jesus came looking for sinners and the lost, folks just
like us. God loves us, forgives us, and grants us the power of
the Spirit to live a new life filled with forgiveness for others
and truth for ourselves.

22

Prayers of the People (and the Lord's Prayer)

O God, who dwells in the light so deep it is darkness to us, we come to worship you. You, who dwell among the fairest of heaven and outshine them all, we come to offer you our praises. You, who are all holiness, invite us to worship you and commune with you. We who are sinful but dust of the earth, look at each other in judgment.

(The following paragraph may be used if a separate prayer of confession has not been used.)
We confess to you, O God, and before one another that we have sinned. We have not lived out of your Spirit of forgiveness and acceptance but rather have demonized others while overlooking our own sins. We confess that we are sinners. No one this week mistook us for you. We have much to learn and to become. Forgive us and empower us with your Spirit that we may truly accept others as we become more and more like our Savior.

We give you thanks for all the ways in which you show your acceptance of us and the blessings with which you grace us. You grant us life that is eternal in quality as well as length. You grant us your own Spirit and call us your children.

(Other thanksgivings may be offered.)
We offer up to you the sufferings of our sisters and brothers both far and near. Some of them we know personally. Some we don't know at all. Yet all are your precious children whom Jesus comes to seek.

(Other intercessions may be offered.)
All these things we ask in the name of our Savior Jesus Christ, who taught us to pray together, saying:
Our Father... Amen.

(Or if the Lord's Prayer is not used at this point in the service)
All this we ask in the name of the Blessed and Holy Trinity.
Amen.

Advent 4

Micah 5:2-5a
Hebrews 10:5-10
Luke 1:39-45 (46-55)

Call to Worship
Leader: Let our spirit magnify our God.
People: Let our spirits rejoice in God our Savior.
Leader: God has looked upon us with favor.
People: God is doing great things for us.
Leader: God comes to bring justice to the earth.
People: We welcome God's work and pledge to join it.

OR

Leader: Come let us worship the God who is with us!
People: We come to worship God incarnate.
Leader: God comes to bring salvation and justice to the earth.
People: We come to join in solidarity with God's cause.
Leader: Jesus brings the reign of God among us.
People: We come to make that reign complete through our Christ.

Hymns and Sacred Songs
"Lift Up Your Heads, Ye Mighty Gates"
found in:

UMH: 213	CH: 129
H82: 436	LBW: 32
PH: 8	Renew: 59
NCH: 117	

"Break Forth, O Beauteous Heavenly Light"
found in:
UMH: 223   PH: 26
H82: 91   NCH: 140

"My Soul Gives Glory to My God"
found in:
UMH: 198   CH: 130

"Tell Out, My Soul"
found in:
UMH: 200   Renew: 130
H82: 437/438

"People, Look East"
found in:
UMH: 202   CH: 142
PH: 12

"Hail to the Lord's Anointed"
found in:
UMH: 203   CH: 140
H82: 616   LBW: 87
AAHH: 187   Renew: 101
NCH: 104

"Toda la Tierra" ("All Earth Is Waiting")
found in:
UMH: 210   NCH: 121

"O Come, O Come, Emmanuel"
found in:
UMH: 211   NNBH: 82
H82: 56   NCH: 116

PH: 9   CH: 119
AAHH: 188   LBW: 34

"Your Loving Kindness Is Better than Life"
found in:
CCB: 26

"All Hail King Jesus"
found in:
CCB: 29   Renew: 35

Prayer for the Day / Collect
O God, who loves us enough to become one of us, grant us
the desire to love you enough to become more like you in
our acts of justice and mercy; through Jesus Christ our Savior. Amen.

OR

We come to worship the God who becomes flesh. We come
to sing praises and glory to the God who comes to bring justice and peace to all the earth. So fill us with your Spirit that
our words may become our deeds. Amen.

Prayer of Confession
Leader: Let us confess to God and before one another our
sins and especially our tendency to make Christmas all senti-
ment and to forget God's great purpose.
**People: We confess to you, O God, and before one anoth-
er that we have sinned. We have looked to our relationship with you as one that gives us privilege and special
status. We so easily forget that you have called us to serve
others and bring your reign of justice and peace to its fulfillment. Forgive us our blindness and self-centered ways**

and empower us with your Spirit to enter once more into the way of Jesus and serve the good of others. Amen.
Leader: God desires the full salvation of all creation. God welcomes all to join in the path of Jesus that leads to the wholeness of all of us. God forgives us and welcomes us on the path.

Prayers of the People (and the Lord's Prayer)
We worship and adore you, O God, the Creator of the universe who cares for even the smallest sparrow that falls. You know the travails and trials of your children, and you strive to correct the injustices that we inflict on one another.

(The following paragraph may be used if a separate prayer of confession has not been used.)
We confess to you, O God, and before one another that we have sinned. We have looked to our relationship with you as one that gives us privilege and special status. We so easily forget that you have called us to serve others and bring your reign of justice and peace to its fulfillment. Forgive us our blindness and our self-centered ways and empower us with your Spirit to enter once more into the way of Jesus and serve the good of others.

We give you thanks for all the glorious blessings of this life. We thank you for family and friends, and for those you place before us so that we may share in your work of salvation.

(Other thanksgivings may be offered.)
We pray for one another in our need and for all your children who are yearning for your reign. We pray for those who are oppressed in body, mind, or spirit. We pray for those who are oppressed because of our thoughtless activities and inaction. We pray that we might truly be your people in this world so that this becomes your reign.

28

(Other intercessions may be offered.)
All these things we ask in the name of our Savior Jesus
Christ, who taught us to pray together, saying:
Our Father... Amen.

(Or if the Lord's Prayer is not used at this point in the service)
All this we ask in the name of the Blessed and Holy Trinity.
Amen.

Christmas Eve / Day

Isaiah 9:2-7
Titus 2:11-14
Luke 2:1-14 (15-20)

Call to Worship
Leader: O sing to God a new song;
People: sing to God, all the earth.
Leader: Sing to God, bless God's name;
People: tell of God's salvation from day to day.
Leader: Declare God's glory among the nations,
People: God's marvelous works among all the peoples.

OR

Leader: God has come to be one of us!
People: Thanks be to the incarnate God of love!
Leader: God comes to share our pains and our joys.
People: Thanks be to the God who knows us.
Leader: God comes to be present through us!
People: May our lives reflect the presence of our God!

Hymns and Sacred Songs
"Love Came Down at Christmas"
found in:
UMH: 242   NCH: 165
H82: 84

"Infant Holy, Infant Lowly"
found in:
UMH: 229   LBW: 44
PH: 37   ELW: 276
CH: 163

"What Child Is This"
found in:

UMH: 219	NCH: 148
H82: 115	CH: 162
PH: 53	LBW: 40
AAHH: 220	ELW: 296
NNBH: 86	

"O Little Town of Bethlehem"
found in:

UMH: 230	NCH: 133
H82: 78/79	CH: 144
PH: 43/44	LBW: 41
AAHH: 204	ELW: 279
NNBH: 90	

"While Shepherds Watched Their Flocks"
found in:

UMH: 236	NNBH: 92
H82: 94/95	CH: 154
PH: 58/59	

"Silent Night, Holy Night"
found in:

UMH: 239	NCH: 134
H82: 111	CH: 145
PH: 60	LBW: 65
AAHH: 211	ELW: 281
NNBH: 101	

"The First Noel"
found in:

UMH: 245	NCH: 139
H82: 109	CH: 151

PH: 56 LBW: 56
NNBH: 89 ELW: 300

"Joy to the World"
found in:
UMH: 246 NCH: 132
H82: 100 CH: 143
PH: 40 LBW: 39
AAHH: 197 ELW: 267
NNBH: 94

"Arise, Shine"
found in:
CCB: 2 Renew: 123

"All Hail King Jesus"
found in:
CCB: 29 Renew: 35

Prayer for the Day / Collect
O God, who has chosen to come among us as one of us, grant us the faith to trust in your loving presence not just at Christmas but throughout our lives; through Jesus Christ our Savior. Amen.

OR

We come to celebrate the miracle of God becoming flesh, not just once but forever. God is in our midst as the Spirit fills us and creation with love and grace. Amen.

Prayer of Confession
Leader: Let us confess to God and before one another our sins and especially our failure to see God's incarnate presence in our world.

People: We confess to you, O God, and before one another that we have sinned. Even as we celebrate your incarnation, we are blind to all the ways you have come into creation and into our lives. We miss you in the faces of strangers and in the faces of friends. We miss you in the kindness of others and in the needs of others. Forgive us our blindness and help us to not only celebrate the birth of the Christ Child in Bethlehem so long ago but to celebrate your coming into the world this day and every day. Amen.

Leader: God has and God does come among us. God comes in love to claim us and all creation as his own. Rejoice in God's presence, love, and forgiveness.

Prayers of the People (and the Lord's Prayer)

Praise and glory to you, O God, for your love that brings you into our world. As we praise you for the birth of the Christ Child, we also praise you for your presence in those around us.

(The following paragraph may be used if a separate prayer of confessions has not been used.)

We confess to you, O God, and before one another that we have sinned. Even as we celebrate your incarnation, we are blind to all the ways you have come into creation and into our lives. We miss you in the faces of strangers and in the faces of friends. We miss you in the kindness of others and in the needs of others. Forgive us our blindness and help us to not only celebrate the birth of the Christ Child in Bethlehem so long ago but to celebrate your coming into the world this day and every day.

We give you thanks for Jesus and the ways we are able to see in him what it means for a human being to truly be your child. We thank you for all those throughout history and throughout our lives who have allowed you to be present to the world through them.

(Other thanksgivings may be offered.)
We pray for one another in our need. We pray for those who find it difficult to realize you are with them in their needs. We ask that you would give us the grace to allow you to be present to them through us.

(Other intercessions may be offered.)
All these things we ask in the name of our Savior Jesus Christ, who taught us to pray together, saying:
Our Father... Amen.

(Or if the Lord's Prayer is not used at this point in the service.)
All this we ask in the name of the Blessed and Holy Trinity. Amen.

Christmas 1

1 Samuel 2:18-20, 26
Colossians 3:12-17
Luke 2:41-52

Call to Worship
Leader: Praise God from the heavens;
People: praise God from the heights!
Leader: Praise God, all angels and heavenly host!
People: Praise God, sun, moon, and all stars.
Leader: Praise God, all creatures.
People: Praise God who is the faithful one.

OR

Leader: Come let us praise our God.
People: We come tired and worn out from Christmas.
Leader: Come and find in God your true meaning and new life.
People: We come confused and let down.
Leader: God calls all the children of earth to gather.
People: We come to praise God and rest in God's love for all.

Hymns and Sacred Songs
"Love Came Down at Christmas"
found in:
UMH: 242   NCH: 165
H82: 84

"That Boy-Child of Mary"
found in:
UMH: 241   PH: 55

"Morning Glory, Starlit Sky"
found in:
UMH: 194   H82: 585

"Ye Who Claim the Faith of Jesus"
found in:
UMH: 197   H82: 268/269

"Help Us Accept Each Other"
found in:
UMH: 560   NCH: 388
PH: 358   CH: 487

"From All that Dwell Below the Skies"
found in:
UMH: 101   NCH: 27
H82: 380   CH: 49
PH: 229

"God, Whose Love Is Reigning O'er Us"
found in:
UMH: 100

"All Creatures of Our God and King"
found in:
UMH: 62   NCH: 17
H82: 400   CH: 22
PH: 455   LBW: 257
AAHH: 147   Renew: 47
NNBH: 33

"I Am Loved"
found in:
CCB: 80

"They'll Know We Are Christians By Our Love"
found in:
CCB: 78

Prayer for the Day / Collect

O God, who created us all in your image and filled us with your own life-breath, grant us to know that in you we have life and meaning and that in you we are connected to all your creation; through Jesus Christ our Savior. Amen.

OR

We come to praise you our God and our salvation. We come to find in you the true meaning for our lives that the gifts and the tinsel did not supply. We come together as your people to find your love incarnate once again. Receive our praise and fill our hearts. Amen.

Prayer of Confession

Leader: Let us confess to God and before one another our sins and especially the ways in which we have allowed the celebration of Christmas to drain us and distract us from its true message.

People: We confess to you, O God, and before one another that we have sinned. We have turned the celebration of your coming among us and becoming flesh into a tiring ritual of rushing, shopping, and overindulging. We have missed much of your message of love that became incarnate. We dress children up in cute shepherd costumes and miss the obvious message that the lowest outcasts are part of your good news. Forgive us and empower us with your Spirit to reclaim the glad tidings and share them with all your children. Amen.

Leader: God came in love to claim us and comes today to claim us as well. In the love of God you are forgiven and blessed to be a blessing to all creation.

Prayers of the People (and the Lord's Prayer)
We have come to adore you, O God, as you come among us this day. We have celebrated the feast of the incarnation and are finding ourselves aware that you are still becoming flesh in and among us. You are truly a gracious and loving God.

(The following paragraph may be used if a separate prayer of confession has not been used.)
We confess to you, O God, and before one another that we have sinned. We have turned the celebration of your coming among us and becoming flesh into a tiring ritual of rushing, shopping, and overindulging. We have missed much of your message of love that became incarnate. We dress children up in cute shepherd costumes and miss the obvious message that the lowest outcasts are part of your good news. Forgive us and empower us with your Spirit to reclaim the glad tidings and share them with all your children.

We give you thanks for all the ways you make your love and presence known to us from the glory of creation in all its wondrous expansiveness to the glory of the birth of one little baby. We have been warmed by the love and generosity of others. We have felt the glow of your love even in the midst of our busyness.

(Other thanksgivings may be offered.)
We know that for many this season is a hardship. They are painfully aware of loneliness and need. Many struggle with depression, grief, and despair. Help us to be your presence incarnate to those around us who desperately need to know your love more fully in their lives.

(Other intercessions may be offered.)
All these things we ask in the name of our Savior Jesus Christ, who taught us to pray together, saying:
Our Father... Amen.

(Or if the Lord's Prayer is not used at this point in the service)
All this we ask in the name of the Blessed and Holy Trinity. Amen.

New Year's Day

Ecclesiastes 3:1-13
Revelation 21:1-6a
Matthew 25:31-46

Call to Worship
Leader: O God, our sovereign, how majestic is your name in all the earth!
People: You have set your glory above the heavens.
Leader: When I look at your heavens, the work of your fingers,
People: the moon and the stars that you have established;
Leader: what are human beings that you are mindful of them,
People: mortals that you care for them?
Leader: Yet you have made them a little lower than God
People: and crowned them with glory and honor.

OR

Leader: Come and give thanks for the year gone by.
People: We give God thanks for the blessings we have received.
Leader: Come and give thanks for the year to come.
People: We give God thanks for new opportunities.
Leader: Come and commit your lives to Christ once again.
People: We offer ourselves to our Christ.

Hymns and Sacred Songs
"This Is a Day of New Beginnings"
found in:

UMH: 383   CH: 518
NCH: 417

"God of the Ages"
found in:
UMH: 698   NCH: 592
PH: 262   CH: 725

"O God, Our Help in Ages Past"
found in:
UMH: 117   NCH: 25
H82: 680   CH: 67
AAHH: 170   LBW: 320
NNBH: 46   ELW: 632

"Now Thank We All Our God"
found in:
UMH: 102   NCH: 419
H82: 396/397   CH: 715
PH: 555   LBW: 533/534
NNBH: 330   ELW: 839/840

"Seek Ye First"
found in:
UMH: 405   PH: 333
H82: 711   CH: 354

"Make Me a Captive, Lord"
found in:
UMH: 421   PH: 378

"Let There Be Peace on Earth"
found in:
UMH: 431   CH: 677

"Be Thou My Vision"
found in:
UMH: 451   CH: 595
H82: 488   ELW: 793
PH: 339   Renew: 151
NCH: 451

"As the Deer"
found in:
CCB: 83   Renew: 9

"Refiner's Fire"
found in:
CCB: 79

Prayer for the Day / Collect

O God, who makes all things new, grant us the grace to name Jesus our Savior as we begin this year as his disciples; through Jesus Christ our Savior. Amen.

OR

We come to rejoice in the one who creates and recreates us. You, O God, are the beginning of all life. Help us this year to proclaim Jesus as our Savior as we follow him. Amen.

Prayer of Confession

Leader: Let us confess to God and before one another our sins and especially our reluctance to give up the comfort of who we are in order to become who we are meant to become.

People: We confess to you, O God, and before one another that we have sinned. We look around us at others and decide we are at least as good as others. We avoid looking at Jesus and measuring our lives by his. We are content

to be a little better than other sinners rather than allow-ing the Spirit to form us into your image, into the likeness of our Christ. Forgive us and make us bold to claim the power of your Spirit that dwells within us and is able to transform us into reflections of you. Amen.

Leader: God has given us the power of the Spirit and the incarnate Christ so that we can truly be God's children. Re-ceive the forgiveness and the power God desires us to have. Become who God created you to be.

Prayers of the People (and the Lord's Prayer)

We worship and praise you, O eternal one, who is beyond time and yet dwells within it with us.

(The following paragraph may be used if a separate prayer of confession has not been used.)

We confess to you, O God, and before one another that we have sinned. We look around us at others and decide we are at least as good as others. We avoid looking at Jesus and measuring our lives by his. We are content to be a little bet-ter than other sinners rather than allowing the Spirit to form us into your image, into the likeness of our Christ. Forgive us and make us bold to claim the power of your Spirit that dwells within us and is able to transform us into reflections of you.

We give you thanks for your presence in our lives and especially in these times when we mark the movement of our lives through the years. We thank you for Jesus who came that we might have life and who showed us how to live as your true children.

(Other thanksgivings may be offered.)

We pray for one another in our need and for all your chil-dren. We pray for those who do not know they are loved and adored as your beloved ones. We pray for those who suffer and can see little beyond their pain. We pray for your world as we enter a new year. May we be your presence in a loving and caring way that those around us may know you are here.

(Other intercessions may be offered.)
All these things we ask in the name of our Savior Jesus Christ, who taught us to pray together, saying:
Our Father... Amen.

(Or if the Lord's Prayer is not used at this point in the service)
All this we ask in the name of the Blessed and Holy Trinity. Amen.

Epiphany of Our Lord

Isaiah 60:1-6
Ephesians 3:1-12
Matthew 2:1-12

Call to Worship
Leader: Praise God, you God's people!
People: For God grants us peace.
Leader: God gives snow like wool
People: and frost like ashes.
Leader: God sends out the word!
People: God declares the word to us!

OR

Leader: Come and worship the giver of life.
People: It is from God alone that life comes.
Leader: Come and worship the one who gives meaning to our lives.
People: In God alone we know who we are.
Leader: God is the source of all that is good.
People: Let us rejoice in God's good gifts.

Hymns and Sacred Songs
"Go, Tell It on the Mountain"
found in:

UMH: 251	NNBH: 92
H82: 99	NCH: 154
PH: 29	CH: 167
AAHH: 202	LBW: 70

"O Morning Star, How Fair and Bright"
found in:

UMH: 247   CH: 105
PH: 69   LBW: 76
NCH: 158

"All Praise to Thee, for Thou, O King Divine"
found in:
UMH: 166   H82: 477

"God Created Heaven and Earth"
found in:
UMH: 151   NCH: 33
PH: 292

"Something Beautiful"
found in:
UMH: 394   CCB: 84

"People Need the Lord"
found in:
CCB: 52

Prayer for the Day / Collect
O God, who created us and gives us life eternal, abundant, and joyful, grant us the wisdom to find in you the true meaning of our lives; through Jesus Christ our Savior. Amen.

OR

We come together for worship that we may praise you and learn your ways, our Creator and our redeemer. Bless us in our worship and fill us with your wisdom that we may follow you all the days of our lives and find in you the true meaning of who we are. Amen.

Prayer of Confession

Leader: Let us confess to God and before one another our sins and especially the ways we have looked for life's meaning apart from God.

People: We confess to you, O God, and before one another that we have sinned. We received life from you, and yet we look to others to give our lives meaning. We think that gathering the good things of creation around us will give meaning to our lives. We think that the good opinion of other creatures will give meaning to our lives. We forget that it is only in you that we can discover true life. Forgive our foolishness and heal our blindness that we may once again see you as the giver of all that matters. Amen.

Leader: The giver of every good and perfect gift desires nothing more than to give you abundant, eternal life. As you turn to God, you will find that life is given to you once again.

Prayers of the People (and the Lord's Prayer)

We worship and adore you, O God, because you are the Creator. All that we have and all that we are come as gifts from your beneficent hand. You are life, and our life is totally based on yours.

(The following paragraph may be used if a separate prayer of confession has not been used.)

We confess to you, O God, and before one another that we have sinned. We received life from you, and yet we look to others to give our lives meaning. We think that gathering the good things of creation around us will give meaning to our lives. We think that the good opinion of other creatures will give meaning to our lives. We forget that it is only in you that we can discover true life. Forgive our foolishness and heal our blindness that we may once again see you as the giver of all that matters.

We give you thanks for the abundance of life that is all around us. We thank you for the wonders of the universe that stretches out in proportions beyond our wildest imaginations. We thank you for the wonder of life so small we cannot see it with the naked eye. Most of all, we thank you for Jesus, who brings us your own life back into our existence.

(Other thanksgivings may be offered.)
We offer to your great love and kindness the hurts of our world. Many of these hurts we have imposed on one another. Now we ask that you use our prayers and our joining with your love to be part of the healing of the nations.

(Other intercessions may be offered.)
All these things we ask in the name of our Savior Jesus Christ, who taught us to pray together, saying:
Our Father... Amen.

(Or if the Lord's Prayer is not used at this point in the service)
All this we ask in the name of the Blessed and Holy Trinity. Amen.

Baptism of Our Lord
Epiphany 1
Ordinary Time 1

Isaiah 43:1-7
Acts 8:14-17
Luke 3:15-17, 21-22

Call to Worship
Leader: Ascribe to God glory and strength.
People: Ascribe to God the glory due to God.
Leader: The voice of God is powerful;
People: the voice of God is full of majesty.
Leader: May God give strength to the people!
People: May God bless us with peace!

OR

Leader: Come to God and do not fear.
People: How can we not be afraid?
Leader: The God who created you calls you by name.
People: Can it be that God truly loves us?
Leader: God desires nothing more than to love us and be loved by us.
People: That is all that matters! There is nothing to fear!

Hymns and Sacred Songs
"Be Still, My Soul"
found in:
UMH: 163   NCH: 488
AAHH: 135   CH: 566
NNBH: 263

"Through It All"
found in:
UMH: 507   CH: 555
NNBH: 402

"Give to the Winds Thy Fears"
found in:
UMH: 129   PH: 286

"All My Hope Is Firmly Grounded"
found in:
UMH: 132   NCH: 408
H82: 665   CH: 88

"God Will Take Care of You"
found in:
UMH: 130   NNBH: 52
AAHH: 137   NCH: 460

"On Eagle's Wings"
found in:
UMH: 143   Renew: 112
CH: 77   CCB: 97

"Leaning on the Everlasting Arms"
found in:
UMH: 133   NCH: 471
AAHH: 371   CH: 560
NNBH: 262

"Out of the Depths I Cry to You"
found in:
UMH: 515   NCH: 483
H82: 666   CH: 510
PH: 240   LBW: 295

"Be Not Afraid"
found in:
Renew: 243

"Shine, Jesus, Shine"
found in:
CCB: 81   Renew: 247

Prayer for the Day / Collect

O God, who created us for yourself, grant us the courage to leave our fears behind and to live as your children always; through Jesus Christ our Savior. Amen.

OR

We have come to worship the one who created us to be in communion with the divine. Created in your image, you call us to rest in the assurance that we are held in your hand. Cast out our fear and give us the courage to live as Jesus' disciples. Amen.

Prayer of Confession

Leader: Let us confess to God and before one another our sins and especially how easily we forget that we are God's own people.

People: We confess to you, O God, and before one another that we have sinned. We are created in your image and have been claimed by you to be your people, and yet we so easily forget our place in your realm. We find ourselves surrounded by many unsettling events and fear grips our hearts. We allow many temporal concerns to rob us of our birthright as your children. We fear that we will lose our dignity and sense of worth if we lose our jobs, our money, or our position in society. We forget that the only true dignity comes from you and that you have

declared us to be of infinite worth to you. Forgive us and restore us in your Spirit to a life of courage and discipleship. Amen.

Leader: God comes to us so that we need not fear. Know that God still loves us and claims us. Live in the sanctuary of God's love.

Prayers of the People (and the Lord's Prayer)

We worship and offer our praises to you, the Creator of all, the Creator of us all. You who created the far reaches of space have created us in your own image and endowed us with reason and thought. You have given us your very own life, breath, and Spirit.

(The following paragraph may be used if a separate prayer of confession has not been used.)

We confess to you, O God, and before one another that we have sinned. We are created in your image and have been claimed by you to be your people, and yet we so easily forget our place in your realm. We find ourselves surrounded by many unsettling events, and fear grips our hearts. We allow many temporal concerns to rob us of our birthright as your children. We fear that we will lose our dignity and sense of worth if we lose our jobs, our money, or our position in society. We forget that the only true dignity comes from you and that you have declared us to be of infinite worth to you. Forgive us and restore us in your Spirit to a life of courage and discipleship.

We give you thanks for the gift of your love, which created us and makes us your own people. You have gifted us with your love and care and have made us in your own image.

(Other thanksgivings may be offered.)

We pray for one another in our need and for all your children around the world. We pray especially for those who do not know the joy of your love and care.

(Other intercessions may be offered.)
All these things we ask in the name of our Savior Jesus Christ, who taught us to pray together, saying:
Our Father... Amen.

(Or if the Lord's Prayer is not used at this point in the service)
All this we ask in the name of the Blessed and Holy Trinity. Amen.

Epiphany 2
Ordinary Time 2

Isaiah 62:1-5
1 Corinthians 12:1-11
John 2:1-11

Call to Worship
Leader: The steadfast love of God extends to the heavens.
People: The faithfulness of God extends to the clouds.
Leader: God's righteousness is like the mighty mountains.
People: God's judgments are like the great deep.
Leader: With God is the fountain of light.
People: In God's light, we see light.

OR

Leader: We come to God desolate and forsaken.
People: We are a broken and dying people.
Leader: God comes to give us a new name.
People: God comes and we are no longer forsaken.
Leader: God comes to bring us light and life.
People: In God alone we find life in all its fullness.

Hymns and Sacred Songs
"God Created Heaven and Earth"
found in:
UMH: 151   NCH: 33
PH: 290

"Morning Has Broken"
found in:
UMH: 145   PH: 469
H82: 8   CH: 53

"This Is a Day of New Beginnings"
found in:
UMH: 383   CH: 518
NCH: 417

"Spirit of the Living God"
found in:
UMH: 393   NCH: 283
PH: 322   CH: 295
AAHH: 320   CCB: 57
NNBH: 133   Renew: 90

"Something Beautiful"
found in:
UMH: 394   CCB: 84

"O Come and Dwell in Me"
found in:
UMH: 388

"Love Divine, All Loves Excelling"
found in:
UMH: 384   NCH: 43
H82: 657   CH: 517
PH: 376   LBW: 315
AAHH: 440   Renew: 196
NNBH: 65

"Change My Heart, O God"
found in:
CCB: 56   Renew: 143

Prayer for the Day / Collect

O God, who has created us and so wonderfully redeemed us,
grant us the faith to trust in your love enough to allow you

to change us into the glory you have in store for us; through Jesus Christ our Savior. Amen.

OR

We come into God's presence and celebrate the love that brings us light and life. We come in need of God's grace and healing and we find both in abundance. Open our hearts to your love, O God, that we may know more fully the joy of living in your image. Amen.

Prayer of Confession
Leader: Let us confess to God and before one another our sins and especially the way we cling to the old ways that lead to death.
People: We confess to you, O God, and before one another that we have sinned. We have failed to trust you with our lives. We have held on to our own ideas of who we should be, and we have missed the glory that you have in mind for us. We have settled for stability that leads to stagnation and death, instead of accepting the change you bring that leads to transformation and life eternal. Forgive us and renew your vision within us that we may receive your Spirit and the transformation you bring. Amen.
Leader: God loves and delights in nothing more than seeing us grow and mature into the vibrant people we are meant to become. Know that God's Spirit is always offered to those who will receive. Receive and change.

Prayers of the People (and the Lord's Prayer)
We worship and praise your name, O God, for you are the one who created us and who has the vision of who we can become. We praise you for your wisdom, your vision, and your gracious love.

(The following paragraph may be used if a separate prayer of confession has not been used.)
We confess to you, O God, and before one another that we have sinned. We have failed to trust you with our lives. We have held on to our own ideas of who we should be, and we have missed the glory that you have in mind for us. We have settled for stability that leads to stagnation and death, instead of accepting the change you bring that leads to transformation and life eternal. Forgive us and renew your vision within us that we may receive your Spirit and the transformation you bring.

We thank you for all the ways you make known to us the glory that awaits us as you transform us more fully into your image. Most of all we thank you for Jesus, who lived among us as one of us filled with your glory, grace, and Spirit.

(Other thanksgivings may be offered.)
We pray for one another in our need and especially for those who find this world so far from what you desire it to be. Grant that we may become more full of you so that we may be used as you fill the whole world with your presence.

(Other intercessions may be offered.)
All these things we ask in the name of our Savior Jesus Christ, who taught us to pray together, saying:
Our Father... Amen.

(Or if the Lord's Prayer is not used at this point in the service)
All this we ask in the name of the Blessed and Holy Trinity. Amen.

Epiphany 3
Ordinary Time 3

Nehemiah 8:1-3, 5-6, 8-10
1 Corinthians 12:12-31a
Luke 4:14-21

Call to Worship
Leader: The heavens are telling the glory of God.
People: The firmament proclaims God's handiwork.
Leader: Day to day pours forth speech,
People: and night to night declares knowledge.
Leader: The way of our God is perfect;
People: God's ways revive our souls.

OR

Leader: God calls to the children of earth to gather.
People: We have gathered to worship and praise our God.
Leader: We come from many places, many races, many clans.
People: Yet we are all God's handiwork, all God's children.
Leader: Different as we are, we need one another to be whole.
People: Only as we gather all God's children do we find shalom.

Hymns and Sacred Songs
"Jesus, United By Thy Grace"
found in:
UMH: 561

"Help Us Accept Each Other"
found in:
UMH: 560   NCH: 388
PH: 358   CH: 487

"Christ Is Made the Sure Foundation"
found in:
UMH: 559   NCH: 400
H82: 518   CH: 275
PH: 416/417   LBW: 367

"Where Charity and Love Prevail"
found in:
UMH: 549   CH: 275
H82: 581   LBW: 367
NCH: 400

"O Church of God, United"
found in:
UMH: 547

"In Christ There Is No East or West"
found in:
UMH: 548   NNBH: 299
H82: 529   NCH: 394/395
PH: 439/440   CH: 387
AAHH: 398/399   LBW: 259

"The Church's One Foundation"
found in:
UMH: 545/546   NNBH: 297
H82: 526   NCH: 386
PH: 442   CH: 272
AAHH: 337   LBW: 369

"God, Whose Love Is Reigning O'er Us"
found in:
UMH: 100

"I Am Loved"
found in:
CCB: 80

"Unity"
found in:
CCB: 59

Prayer for the Day / Collect
O God, who created all humanity from the dust of the earth and the breath of your being, grant us the wisdom to know that we belong together as the parts of our body all belong to one another; through Jesus Christ our Savior. Amen.

OR

We have come to worship you, our Creator God, who has made us all in your image. You have made us who we are and we rejoice in your loving care. Draw us close to you and one another that we may reflect your unity and your love. Amen.

Prayer of Confession
Leader: Let us confess to God and before one another our sins and especially the way we have placed divisions within the body of Christ.
People: We confess to you, O God, and before one another that we have sinned. We have failed to be your faithful people in the way we have excluded those whom you seek to include. We have chosen based on human compatibility rather than on the basis of your never-ending love. We

have chosen based on our preferences rather than your grace. Forgive us and open our eyes to the worth of all your creatures. Amen.
Leader: God loves us all and invites us to come together into the love and grace that never fails.

Prayers of the People (and the Lord's Prayer)
We worship and adore the one who has made us in all our complex diversity. All creation speaks of the wonderful variety that works together to make creation sing.

(The following paragraph may be used if a separate prayer of confession has not been used.)
We confess to you, O God, and before one another that we have sinned. We have failed to be your faithful people in the ways in which we have excluded those whom you seek to include. We have chosen based on human compatibility rather than on the basis of your never-ending love. We have chosen based on our preferences rather than your grace. Forgive us and open our eyes to the worth of all your creatures.

We give you thanks for all those who are a part of us and our lives. We thank you for those who have abilities and talents that we do not. We thank you for our place and theirs in your great salvation adventure.

(Other thanksgivings may be offered.)
We pray for those who do not feel a connection to you or to your people. Help us to share your love in more visible and concrete ways so that all may know your redeeming love.

(Other intercessions may be offered.)
All these things we ask in the name of our Savior Jesus Christ, who taught us to pray together, saying:
Our Father... Amen.

Epiphany 4
Ordinary Time 4

Jeremiah 1:4-10
1 Corinthians 13:1-13
Luke 4:21-30

Call to Worship
Leader: In you, O God, we take refuge.
People: Let us never be put to shame.
Leader: In your righteousness, deliver and rescue us.
People: Be to us a rock of refuge, a strong fortress.
Leader: For you, O God, are our hope and trust.
People: Our praise is continually of you.

OR

Leader: Draw near and hear a word from our God.
People: We would like to hear a word of comfort from God.
Leader: It may be comfort, it may be correction.
People: Why does God correct us?
Leader: God corrects us to bring us to life eternal.
People: Let us listen for God's word to us.

Hymns and Sacred Songs
"Tu Has Venado a la Orilla" ("Lord, You Have Come to the Lakeshore")
found in:
UMH: 344   CH: 342
PH: 377

"The Voice of God Is Calling"
found in:
UMH: 436   CH: 666

"Jesus Calls Us"
found in:
UMH: 398   NCH: 171/172
H82: 549/550   CH: 337
NNBH: 183   LBW: 494

"Stand Up, Stand Up for Jesus"
found in:
UMH: 514   NNBH: 409
H82: 561   CH: 613
AAHH: 476   LBW: 389

"Behold a Broken World"
found in:
UMH: 426

"Cuando el Pobre" ("When the Poor Ones")
found in:
UMH: 434   CH: 662
PH: 401

"The Gift of Love"
found in:
UMH: 408   CH: 526
AAHH: 522   Renew: 155

"Make Me a Servant"
found in:
CCB: 90

"As We Gather"
found in:
CCB: 12   Renew: 6

Prayer for the Day / Collect

O God, who calls us to speak and act in your love, grant us the courage and grace to do so even when others despise us for it; through Jesus Christ our Savior. Amen.

OR

We have gathered to receive our marching orders. Fill us with your Spirit and your courage that we may bravely go forth to share your love with all your children. Amen.

Prayer of Confession

Leader: Let us confess to God and before one another our sins and especially the way we shirk our calling because of what others might think of us.

People: We confess to you, O God, and before one another that we have sinned. We have failed you, our neighbors, and ourselves by listening to the voices of those around us instead of to your voice. Call us once more to faithfulness and courage that we may serve you and others more fully and be more true to the image in which you created us. Amen.

Leader: God welcomes all of us wayward sheep back into the fold and gladly allows us to return to the holy task we have been given. May the power of the Spirit give us courage and grace.

Prayers of the People (and the Lord's Prayer)

We bring you our praise and worship, O God, because you are the faithful one who never fails to love us and to seek the good of all your children.

(The following paragraph may be used if a separate prayer of confession has not been used.)
We confess to you, O God, and before one another that we have sinned. We have failed you, our neighbors, and ourselves by listening to the voices of those around us instead of to your voice. Call us once more to faithfulness and courage that we may serve you and others more fully and be more true to the image in which you created us.

We give you thanks for all the ways you have loved us this week. We thank you for the beauty of nature through which you wrapped your arms around us and for the faithful ones who held us in their prayers.

(Other thanksgivings may be offered.)
We lift up to you the cares of our hearts. We pray for those who faithfully carry your love to others and for those who have not yet learned of your love.

(Other intercessions may be offered.)
All these things we ask in the name of our Savior Jesus Christ, who taught us to pray together, saying:
Our Father... Amen.

(Or if the Lord's Prayer is not used at this point in the service)
All this we ask in the name of the Blessed and Holy Trinity. Amen.

Transfiguration of Our Lord
(Last Sunday after Epiphany)

Exodus 34:29-35
2 Corinthians 3:12—4:2
Luke 9:28-36 (37-43)

Call to Worship
Leader: God reigns; let the people tremble!
People: God sits enthroned upon the cherubim.
Leader: God is exalted over all the people.
People: Let us praise God's great and awesome name!
Leader: Extol God and worship at the holy mountain.
People: For our God is great and holy.

OR

Leader: Come into the presence of our God.
People: We come to sing and praise our God.
Leader: God delights in praise but also wants us to listen.
People: We listen to the hymns, the prayers, the readings, and the sermon.
Leader: In these and in much more, listen always for God's voice.
People: We are God's people. We will listen for God's voice.

Hymns and Sacred Songs
"Jesus Calls Us"
found in:
UMH: 398
H82: 549/550
NNBH: 183

NCH: 171/172
CH: 337
LBW: 494

"Be Still, My Soul"
found in:
UMH: 534   NCH: 488
AAHH: 135   CH: 566
NNBH: 263

"Like the Murmur of the Dove's Song"
found in:
UMH: 544   NCH: 270
H82: 513   CH: 245
PH: 314   Renew: 280

"Blessed Jesus, at Thy Word"
found in:
UMH: 596   LBW: 248
H82: 440   Renew: 93
PH: 454

"Wonderful Words of Life"
found in:
UMH: 600   NCH: 319
AAHH: 332   CH: 323
NNBH: 293

"God Hath Spoken By the Prophets"
found in:
UMH: 108   LBW: 238

"God, You Are My God"
found in:
CCB: 60

"Open Our Eyes, Lord"
found in:
CCB: 77   Renew: 91

"Be Still and Know"
found in:
Renew: 10

Prayer for the Day / Collect

O God, who created us for communion with you and one another, grant us the wisdom to listen for you, not only in worship but in all of life that we may learn to walk in your ways; through Jesus Christ our Savior. Amen.

OR

We come to worship and praise our God, but we also come to hear a word from the Lord. Even as God desires to listen to us, we pray for a heart that wants to listen to God that we may learn to be obedient disciples of our Savior, Jesus, in whose name we pray. Amen.

Prayer of Confession

Leader: Let us confess to God and before one another our sins and especially the ways in which we have failed to listen to our God.

People: We confess to you, O God, and before one another that we have sinned. We have tuned our ears to those around us; we have listened to politicians and pundits of all persuasions tell us what to think, and we have failed to listen to you. Open our ears once again that we may hear of your plans for creation and become obedient followers of Jesus. Amen.

Leader: God delights to tell us of his love and desire for our lives. May God's Spirit fill you and speak clearly to you that you may indeed learn obedience.

Prayers of the People (and the Lord's Prayer)

We worship and praise your name, O God, because you have created us to be your companions. As you walked with our first earth parents "in the cool of the day," you desire to walk and talk with us.

(The following paragraph may be used if a separate prayer of confession has not been used.)
We confess to you, O God, and before one another that we have sinned. We have tuned our ears to those around us; we have listened to politicians and pundits of all persuasions tell us what to think, and we have failed to listen to you. Open our ears once again that we may hear of your plans for creation and become obedient followers of Jesus.

We praise you for all the ways you have spoken to us. You have sent us judges, prophets, seers, and psalmists. You have inspired people to collect and write down their words. You have spoken in the majesty of nature, and your glory sings in the silent music of space.

(Other thanksgivings may be offered.)
We pray for one another in our need and especially for those who have no one to listen to them. We know how lonely it can be to be ignored and left out. As Jesus came and listened to the poor, the sinner, and the outcast, help us to listen to one another and to listen to you.

(Other intercessions may be offered.)
All these things we ask in the name of our Savior Jesus Christ, who taught us to pray together, saying:
Our Father... Amen.

(Or if the Lord's Prayer is not used at this point in the service)
All this we ask in the name of the Blessed and Holy Trinity. Amen.

Ash Wednesday

Joel 2:1-2, 12-17
2 Corinthians 5:20b — 6:10
Matthew 6:1-6, 16-21

Call to Worship
Leader: Have mercy on us, O God, according to your steadfast love;
People: according to your abundant mercy, blot out our transgressions.
Leader: Purge us with hyssop, and we shall be clean;
People: wash us, and we shall be whiter than snow.
Leader: Restore to us the joy of your salvation
People: and sustain in us a willing spirit.

OR

Leader: Return to your God, for God is gracious and merciful, slow to anger,
People: and abounding in steadfast love and relents from punishing.
Leader: Gather the people, sanctify the congregation,
People: assemble the aged, gather the children.
Leader: Spare your people, O God!
People: Let us return to God with all our hearts!

Hymns and Sacred Songs
"Lord, Who Throughout These Forty Days"
found in:
UMH: 269   NCH: 211
H82: 142   CH: 180
PH: 81

"Only Trust Him"
found in:
UMH: 337   NNBH: 193
AAHH: 369

"Where He Leads Me"
found in:
UMH: 338   NNBH: 229
AAHH: 550   CH: 346

"Spirit Song"
found in:
UMH: 347   CH: 352
AAHH: 321

"Softly and Tenderly"
found in:
UMH: 348   NCH: 449
AAHH: 347   CH: 340
NNBH: 168   ELW: 608

"Just As I Am, Without One Plea"
found in:
UMH: 357   NCH: 207
H82: 693   CH: 339
PH: 370   LBW: 296
AAHH: 344/345   ELW: 592
NNBH: 167

"Love Divine, All Loves Excelling"
found in:
UMH: 384   NCH: 43
H82: 657   CH: 517
PH: 376   LBW: 315

AAHH: 440   ELW: 631
NNBH: 65

"Jesus Calls Us"
found in:
UMH: 398   CH: 337
H82: 549/550   LBW: 494
NNBH: 183   ELW: 696
NCH: 171/172

"As the Deer"
found in:
CCB: 83   Renew: 9

"Refiner's Fire"
found in:
CCB: 79

Prayer for the Day / Collect

O God, who desires life for your children, grant us the grace to return to you that we may find life abundant and joyful; through Jesus Christ our Savior. Amen.

OR

We come to you, O God, to acknowledge that we are but dust of the earth unless you breathe your life and Spirit into us. May this season of Lent be to us a new beginning as we turn to you and to life eternal. Amen.

Prayer of Confession

Leader: Let us confess to God and before one another our sins and especially our constant wandering from the paths of life to the ways of death.

People: We confess to you, O God, and before one another that we have sinned. You have set before us the way to life eternal and yet we choose paths that lead us to destruction. You made us in your image of love and yet we are able to see others in hunger, pain, and poverty but we do nothing to help. We have failed to be your people. We have failed to act as the body of Christ. Forgive us and return us to your paths that we may join our Savior in reaching out to others in love. Amen.

Leader: God is always calling us back to love and to life. God's is faithful to forgive and redeem. Rejoice in God's love.

Prayers of the People (and the Lord's Prayer)

Praised and wondrous is your name, O God, who has created us and who has redeemed us. We praise your for your loving kindness to all you have created.

(The following paragraph may be used if a separate prayer of confessions has not been used.)

We confess to you, O God, and before one another that we have sinned. You have set before us the way to life eternal and yet we choose paths that lead us to destruction. You made us in your image of love and yet we are able to see others in hunger, pain, and poverty but we do nothing to help. We have failed to be your people. We have failed to act as the body of Christ. Forgive us and return us to your paths that we may join our Savior in reaching out to others in love.

We give you thanks for this time of Lent, which calls us back, once again, to you and to life. We thank you for the faithfulness of the church throughout the ages to call your people to repentance and new life.

(Other thanksgivings may be offered.)

74

We pray for ourselves, your church around the world, and all your creation. Help us, who own the name of Christ, to make this a time of true repentance that we may faithfully be the body of Christ to those around us.

(Other intercessions may be offered.)
All these things we ask in the name of our Savior Jesus Christ, who taught us to pray together, saying:
Our Father... Amen.

(Or if the Lord's Prayer is not used at this point in the service.)
All this we ask in the name of the Blessed and Holy Trinity. Amen.

Lent 1

Deuteronomy 26:1-11
Romans 10:8b-13
Luke 4:1-13

Call to Worship
Leader: God comes among us in our worship.
People: We will draw near and listen to our God.
Leader: God comes among us in our joys.
People: We will draw near and see what God is doing.
Leader: God draws near us in our wilderness experiences.
People: We will draw near and in silence wait on God.

Hymns and Sacred Songs
"Lord, Who Throughout These Forty Days"
found in:
UMH: 269   NCH: 211
H82: 142   CH: 180
PH: 81

"Come Out the Wilderness"
found in:
UMH: 416   AAHH: 367

"Be Still, My Soul"
found in:
UMH: 534   NCH: 488
AAHH: 135   LBW: 566
NNBH: 263

"Stand By Me"
found in:

UMH: 512   CH: 629
NNBH: 318

"Out of the Depths I Cry to You"
found in:
UMH: 515   NCH: 483
H82: 666   CH: 510
PH: 240   LBW: 295

"O Thou, in Whose Presence"
found in:
UMH: 518

"Saranam, Saranam"
found in:
UMH: 523

"Nearer, My God, to Thee"
found in:
UMH: 528   NCH: 606
AAHH: 163   CH: 577
NNBH: 314

"Through It All"
found in:
UMH: 507   CH: 555
NNBH: 402   CCB: 61

"All I Need Is You"
found in:
CCB: 100

"You Are Mine"
found in:
CCB: 58

Prayer for the Day / Collect

O God, who created us for your loving companionship, grant us the grace to be silent in the wilderness time of our lives that we may more clearly perceive your presence among and within us; through Jesus Christ our Savior. Amen.

OR

We have come into your presence, O God, to worship you and to praise your holy name. We have come to offer ourselves to your service as we follow our Savior Jesus. Help us to be willing to enter the wilderness of our lives with him and quietly await what you would reveal to us. Amen.

Prayer of Confession

Leader: Let us confess to God and before one another our sins and especially our tendency to take the easy way out.

People: We confess to you, O God, and before one another that we have sinned. When life gets rough and we become uncomfortable, we forget to seek you and your ways which will lead to life and spiritual growth. Instead, we seek the easy way out. We want to cover over the emptiness and silence, instead of finding you and allowing you to fill the void. Forgive us and grant us the faith to wait in silence for you to speak to us once more your message of life and hope. Amen.

Leader: God is always waiting for us and is always ready to be with us in all of our lives. Know that God loves us, forgives us, and gives us his Spirit to guide us into new life.

Prayers of the People (and the Lord's Prayer)

We praise and adore you, O God, for your steadfast love that never leaves us nor fails us. You are the constant one who never changes and who is closer to us than our own breath.

(The following paragraph may be used if a separate prayer of confession has not been used.)
We confess to you, O God, and before one another that we have sinned. When life gets rough and we become uncomfortable, we forget to seek you and your ways that will lead to life and spiritual growth. Instead, we seek the easy way out. We want to cover over the emptiness and silence, instead of finding you and allowing you to fill the void. Forgive us and grant us the faith to wait in silence for you to speak to us once more your message of life and hope.

We thank you for the ways you communicate your presence to us. We thank you for the way the scripture comes alive with your Spirit and for the times of communion in prayer. We thank you for the sacraments, which become so powerful with your presence. We thank you for all the times you have been with us when we have not even been aware that you were working within us.

(Other thanksgivings may be offered.)
We pray for all, anywhere, who are in the wilderness experience. We pray that as you are with them in that time, they will be aware of you. We ask that you would make us sensitive to those around us so that when they are crossing the desert, we can be there to offer a bit of shade and cup of cool water.

(Other intercessions may be offered.)
All these things we ask in the name of our Savior Jesus Christ, who taught us to pray together, saying:
Our Father... Amen.

(Or if the Lord's Prayer is not used at this point in the service)
All this we ask in the name of the Blessed and Holy Trinity. Amen.

Lent 2

Genesis 15:1-12, 17-18
Philippians 3:17—4:1
Luke 13:31-35

Call to Worship
Leader: God is our light and our salvation;
People: whom shall we fear?
Leader: God is the stronghold of our lives;
People: of whom shall we be afraid?
Leader: One thing we ask of our God;
People: that we may dwell in God's presence always.

OR

Leader: God invites us to come and worship.
People: We come to worship our Creator.
Leader: God invites us to join in creating.
People: We unite with God in building God's reign.
Leader: God calls us to create together.
People: With one another we will serve God and humanity.

Hymns and Sacred Songs
"All Creatures of Our God and King"
found in:
UMH: 62
H82: 400
PH: 455
AAHH: 147
NNBH: 33
NCH: 17
CH: 22
LBW: 527
Renew: 47

"Maker, in Whom We Live"
found in:
UMH: 88

"For the Beauty of the Earth"
found in:
UMH: 92   NCH: 28
H82: 416   CH: 56
PH: 473   LBW: 561
NNBH: 8

"For the Fruits of this Creation"
found in:
UMH: 97   NCH: 425
H82: 424   CH: 714
PH: 553   LBW: 563

"God of the Sparrow, God of the Whale"
found in:
UMH: 122   NCH: 32
PH: 272   CH: 70

"O God of Every Nation"
found in:
UMH: 435   CH: 310
H82: 607   LBW: 416
PH: 289

"Behold a Broken World"
found in:
UMH: 426

"Let There Be Light"
found in:

UMH: 440   CH: 589
NCH: 450

"For the Gift of Creation"
found in:
CCB: 67

"Refiner's Fire"
found in:
CCB: 79

Prayer for the Day / Collect
O God, who created us to be co-creators with you, grant us the wisdom and courage to be part of making the world better rather than just complaining about the state of the world; through Jesus Christ our Savior. Amen.

OR

As you come among us this day, our Creator and redeemer, we offer you our praise and adoration for your creating powers. We ask you to re-create us more fully into your image that we may meaningfully participate in your bringing your creation to the fullness of your dream. Amen.

Prayer of Confession
Leader: Let us confess to God and before one another our sins and especially the ways we are so quick to be critical and so slow to do the work of solving the problem.
People: We confess to you, O God, and before one another that we have sinned. You have created us to join in bringing your creation to its fullness, but we spend most of our time complaining about the way things are without offering any ideas or any help. We want to judge the ways things are, but we don't want to take responsibility

for making it better. Forgive us and send the power of your creating Spirit to fill us and empower us to live into the image you created for us. Amen.

Leader: God desires nothing more than bringing creation to its fullness. When we are willing to be a part of that process, both by being transformed and transforming the world, God joyfully accepts our participation.

Prayers of the People (and the Lord's Prayer)

We praise you, O God, for the wonders of your creating power. We are in awe of the magnitude of creation. We are in awe that you have made us to be your co-creators.

(The following paragraph may be used if a separate prayer of confession has not been used.)

We confess to you, O God, and before one another that we have sinned. You have created us to join in bringing your creation to its fullness, but we spend most of our time complaining about the way things are without offering any ideas or any help. We want to judge the ways things are, but we don't want to take responsibility for making it better. Forgive us and send the power of your creating Spirit to fill us and empower us to live in the image you created for us.

We give you thanks for the power of creation that you have shared with your children. We thank you for our ability to think and analyze and bring forth new thoughts and new solutions. We thank you for the ways we find you in the midst of this process.

(Other thanksgivings may be offered.)

We pray for those who are stuck and find it so difficult to make something worthwhile out of their lives. We pray that as your Spirit works within them to inspire them, you will help us to create the systems and situations where their work can be fruitful.

(Other intercessions may be offered.)
All these things we ask in the name of our Savior Jesus
Christ, who taught us to pray together, saying:
Our Father... Amen.

(Or if the Lord's Prayer is not used at this point in the service)
All this we ask in the name of the Blessed and Holy Trinity.
Amen.

Lent 3

Isaiah 55:1-9
1 Corinthians 10:1-13
Luke 13:1-9

Call to Worship
Leader: Behold the power and glory of our God!
People: God's steadfast love is better than life itself.
Leader: Let us bless God as long as we live.
People: We lift up our hands and call on God's name.
Leader: In the shadow of God's wings, let us sing for joy.
People: We cling to God, whose right hand upholds us.

OR

Leader: Come into the presence of our God.
People: But we are sinful and unfaithful people.
Leader: God knows that and God loves us anyway.
People: We are truly sorry for our unfaithfulness and sin.
Leader: God invites us to not only be sorry but also to be made new.
People: We will turn to God and live as God's children.

Hymns and Sacred Songs
"Dear Lord and Father of Mankind"
found in:

UMH: 358

H82: 652/653

PH: 345

NCH: 502

CH: 594

LBW: 506

"It's Me, It's Me, O Lord"
found in:

UMH: 352
NNBH: 496

CH: 579

"I Surrender All"
found in:
UMH: 354
AAHH: 396

NNBH: 198

"Spirit of the Living God"
found in:
UMH: 393
PH: 322
AAHH: 320
NNBH: 133

NCH: 283
CH: 259
Renew: 90

"Take My Life and Let It Be"
found in:
UMH: 399
H82: 707
PH: 391
NNBH: 213

NCH: 448
CH: 609
LBW: 406
Renew: 150

"Lord, I Want to Be a Christian"
found in:
UMH: 402
PH: 372
AAHH: 463
NNBH: 156

NCH: 454
CH: 589
Renew: 145

"I Want to Walk As a Child of the Light"
found in:
UMH: 206
H82: 490

Renew: 152

"O Master, Let Me Walk with Thee"
found in:

UMH: 430	NCH: 503
H82: 659/660	CH: 602
PH: 357	LBW: 492
NNBH: 445	

"Refiner's Fire"
found in:
CCB: 79

"Change My Heart, O God"
found in:

CCB: 56	Renew: 143

Prayer for the Day / Collect
O God, who calls your children to turn and walk in the way of life, grant us the courage to truly repent, to turn our lives to face you and walk in new paths; through Jesus Christ our Savior. Amen.

OR

We come into your presence, O God, that we may amend our lives and live as Jesus taught and showed us. Amen.

Prayer of Confession
Leader: Let us confess to God and before one another our sins and especially the ease with which we say we are sorry for the things we said and did though we seldom change our way of living.
People: We confess to you, O God, and before one another that we have sinned. We have been unfaithful to you and hurtful to one another. We have said we are sorry when we have had no intention of changing. We have

said we are sorry when we intended to change, but have not changed. **We are more interested in people thinking we are good than we are in actually being good. Forgive us and make us bold to turn our lives around and live fully in your presence. Amen.**

Leader: God desires that we live in wholeness and peace. God welcomes our confession and empowers us with the Spirit to become the children of God we truly are.

Prayers of the People (and the Lord's Prayer)

We raise our voices in praise to you, our God and teacher, for you are the one who lives in wholeness and holiness. Your actions are one with your intentions. You desire that we would live the same way.

(The following paragraph may be used if a separate prayer of confession has not been used.)

We confess to you, O God, and before one another that we have sinned. We have been unfaithful to you and hurtful to one another. We have said we are sorry when we had no intention of changing. We have said we are sorry when we intended to change, but have not changed. We are more interested in people thinking we are good than we are in actually being good. Forgive us and make us bold to turn our lives around and live fully in your presence.

We give you thanks for all the ways you lead us into a full and abundant life. We thank you for the scriptures and the traditions of the church, which help us to understand your desires for us. We thank you for the teachings and life of Jesus and for the Spirit that guides and empowers us.

(Other thanksgivings may be offered.)

We pray for those who find themselves lost in this world without direction. We pray that we may be faithful in following you, so that our lives may serve as a pattern for them.

(Other intercessions may be offered.)
All these things we ask in the name of our Savior Jesus
Christ, who taught us to pray together, saying:
Our Father... Amen.

(Or if the Lord's Prayer is not used at this point in the service)
All this we ask in the name of the Blessed and Holy Trinity.
Amen.

Lent 4

Joshua 5:9-12
2 Corinthians 5:16-21
Luke 15:1-3, 11b-32

Call to Worship
Leader: Happy are we whose transgression is forgiven,
People: happy are we whose sin is covered.
Leader: Let all who are faithful offer prayer to God.
People: Let us listen to the counsel of our God.
Leader: Be glad in God and rejoice, O righteous,
People: and shout for joy, all you upright in heart.

OR

Leader: Come, let us celebrate our prodigal God.
People: God is prodigal? How is that?
Leader: To be prodigal is to be extravagant, free-handed.
People: Then our God is certainly prodigal!
Leader: We are blessed to have a God who gives so freely.
People: Let us thank God and show we are God's children by our liberality.

Hymns and Sacred Songs
"What Wondrous Love Is This"
found in:
UMH: 292   CH: 200
H82: 439   LBW: 385
PH: 85   ELW: 666
NCH: 223

"Lift High the Cross"
found in:

UMH: 159　　　　　　　NCH: 198
H82: 473　　　　　　　CH: 108
PH: 371　　　　　　　 LBW: 377
AAHH: 242　　　　　　ELW: 660

"How Can We Name a Love"
found in:
UMH: 111

"Love Divine, All Loves Excelling"
found in:
UMH: 384　　　　　　　NCH: 43
H82: 657　　　　　　　CH: 517
PH: 376　　　　　　　 LBW: 315
AAHH: 440　　　　　　ELW: 631
NNBH: 65

"O Love Divine, What Hast Thou Done"
found in:
UMH: 287

"The Care the Eagle Gives Her Young"
found in:
UMH: 118　　　　　　　CH: 76
NCH: 468

"O Love, How Deep"
found in:
UMH: 267　　　　　　　NCH: 209
H82: 448/449　　　　　 LBW: 88
PH: 83　　　　　　　　 ELW: 322

"In the Cross of Christ I Glory"
found in:

UMH: 295　　　　　　　NCH: 193/194
H82: 441/442　　　　　LBW: 104
PH: 84　　　　　　　　ELW: 324
NNBH: 104

"I Am Loved"
found in:
CCB: 80

"O How He Love You and Me!"
found in:
CCB: 38　　　　　　　Renew: 27

Prayer for the Day / Collect

O God, who is our prodigal parent, grant us the grace to be as recklessly extravagant with love, grace, and kindness to others as you have been to us; through Jesus Christ our Savior. Amen.

OR

We come into your presence, O God of prodigal love, to offer praise and thanksgiving for your graciousness. We pray that we, too, may be prodigal in giving to others the love, grace, and kindness you have given to us. Amen.

Prayer of Confession

Leader: Let us confess to God and before one another our sins and especially our quickness to receive forgiveness and our slowness to offer it.

People: We confess to you, O God, and before one another that we have sinned. You have been so extravagant with your grace and forgiveness toward us and we have been so slow to forgive others. We remember hurts old and new as if they all happened just yesterday. We assume

that those who have hurt us have done so intentionally, while excusing the things we do against others. Forgive us and so fill us with your Spirit that our forgiveness may be as extravagant and ready as yours. Amen.

Leader: God's forgiveness is extravagant for all, even though we don't deserve it. Receive God's forgiveness and pass it on to others.

Prayers of the People (and the Lord's Prayer)

We worship and adore you, O God, for your abundant, extravagant love that you lavish on all your creation.

(The following paragraph may be used if a separate prayer of confession has not been used.)

We confess to you, O God, and before one another that we have sinned. You have been so extravagant with your grace and forgiveness toward us and we have been so slow to forgive others. We remember hurts old and new as if they all happened just yesterday. We assume that those who have hurt us have done so intentionally, while excusing the things we do against others. Forgive us and so fill us with your Spirit that our forgiveness may be as extravagant and ready as yours.

We thank you for all the ways you have shown us your love. We thank you for creation and for the gift of life. We thank you for your church and its witness to your love. Most of all we thank you for Jesus who brought your love to us in human flesh.

(Other thanksgivings may be offered.)

We pray for one another in our need and for all your children. We know that many find it hard to understand that there is a loving God when life seems so hateful. We pray that we, as your church, may be so faithful to you and your mission that all will soon know the joy of your reign on earth.

(Other intercessions may be offered.)
All these things we ask in the name of our Savior Jesus Christ, who taught us to pray together, saying:
Our Father... Amen.

(Or if the Lord's Prayer is not used at this point in the service)
All this we ask in the name of the Blessed and Holy Trinity. Amen.

Lent 5

Isaiah 43:16-21
Philippians 3:4b-14
John 12:1-8

Call to Worship

Leader: When God restored us, we were like those who dream.

People: Then our mouths were filled with laughter, and our tongues with shouts of joy.

Leader: God has done great things for us and we rejoiced.

People: Restore our fortunes, O God, like the watercourses in the Negeb.

Leader: May those who sow in tears reap with shouts of joy.

People: Those who go out weeping, bearing the seed for sowing, shall come home with shouts of joy, carrying their sheaves.

OR

Leader: Come to God and find your true home.

People: We have tried to come home and we have gotten lost.

Leader: The world has changed. God has opened new paths.

People: We like the old way with which we are comfortable.

Leader: But the old, comfortable ways don't work for those you need to lead to God.

People: We will take the new ways so that we can lead all God's children home.

Hymns and Sacred Songs

"Marching to Zion"
found in:
UMH: 733

"Come, We that Love the Lord"
found in:
UMH: 732   NNBH: 36
H82: 392   NCH: 379/380
AAHH: 590   CH: 707

"Come Sunday"
found in:
UMH: 728

"Arise, Shine Out, Your Light Has Come"
found in:
UMH: 725   Renew: 123
PH: 411

"Happy the Home When God Is There"
found in:
UMH: 445

"We Utter Our Cry"
found in:
UMH: 439

"Let There Be Peace on Earth"
found in:
UMH: 431   CH: 677

"Pues Si Vivimos" ("When We Are Living")
found in:

UMH: 356   CH: 536
PH: 400

"Sanctuary"
found in:
CCB: 87   Renew: 185

"Your Loving Kindness Is Better than Life"
found in:
CCB: 26

Prayer for the Day / Collect

O God, in whom we live and move and have our being, grant us the wisdom and courage to come home to you; through Jesus Christ our Savior. Amen.

OR

We come to worship the one in whom we live and move and have our being. We ask for the power and guidance of the Spirit to help us understand where we are and how we need to go in order to reach home. We pray for the courage to receive new directions. Amen.

Prayer of Confession

Leader: Let us confess to God and before one another our sins and especially the way we cling to old ways that do not work when God is offering us new life.

People: We confess to you, O God, and before one another that we have sinned. Though we are your children and talk about coming to your house for worship, our lives betray our lostness and we seek places other than your presence to fill our lives with meaning. We look to wealth, power, and status, but we also use good things to mask our need for you as we try to substitute family and

friends and good deeds. Help us to understand that it is only in you that we can be the best family member, the best friend, and do the truly good deeds. Amen.
Leader: God is always seeking for his children to return home. Receive the power of God's Spirit as you return to God and begin to shine with the light of God within you.

Prayers of the People (and the Lord's Prayer)
We worship and adore you, the ground of our being and the depth of our lives. From your breath, your Spirit, and your life, we were created. We belong to you and in you.

(The following paragraph may be used if a separate prayer of confession has not been used.)
We confess to you, O God, and before one another that we have sinned. Though we are your children and talk about coming to your house for worship, our lives betray our lostness and we seek places other than your presence to fill our lives with meaning. We look to wealth, power, and status, but we also use good things to mask our need for you as we try to substitute family and friends and good deeds. Help us to understand that it is only in you that we can be the best family member, the best friend, and do the truly good deeds.

We give you thanks for all the ways you have called us to yourself. You have sent us prophets and seers, psalmist and apostles. Most of all, you have sent us Jesus to show us what it means to live in you.

(Other thanksgivings may be offered.)
We pray for those in need and especially for those who are striving to find their home. As you call them to yourself, so fill us with your Spirit that we may be beacons that help them find their way to you.

(Other intercessions may be offered.)

All these things we ask in the name of our Savior Jesus Christ, who taught us to pray together, saying:
Our Father... Amen.

(Or if the Lord's Prayer is not used at this point in the service)
All this we ask in the name of the Blessed and Holy Trinity. Amen.

Passion / Palm Sunday

Isaiah 50:4-9a
Philippians 2:5-11
Luke 22:14—23:56

Call to Worship
Leader: Give thanks to God, for God is good;
People: God's love endures forever.
Leader: Open the gates of righteousness,
People: that we may enter and give thanks.
Leader: This is the day that God has made;
People: we will rejoice and be glad in it.

OR

Leader: Be gracious to us, O God, for we are in distress;
People: our souls and bodies waste away from grief.
Leader: Our lives are spent with sorrows,
People: and our years spent with sighing.
Leader: But we trust in you, O God.
People: We say, "You are our God."

Hymns and Sacred Songs
"Weary of All Trumpeting"
found in:
UMH: 442   H82: 572

"O Young and Fearless Prophet"
found in:
UMH: 444   CH: 669

"Dear Jesus, in Whose Life I See"
found in:
UMH: 468

"Close to Thee"
found in:
UMH: 407   NNBH: 317
AAHH: 552/553

"Seek Ye First"
found in:
UMH: 405   PH: 333
H82: 711   CH: 354

"Take Up Thy Cross"
found in:
UMH: 415   PH: 393
H82: 675   LBW: 398

"Make Me a Captive, Lord"
found in:
UMH: 421   PH: 378

"Take My Life, and Let It Be"
found in:
UMH: 399   NCH: 448
H82: 707   CH: 609
PH: 391   LBW: 406
NNBH: 213   Renew: 150

"Walk with Me"
found in:
CCB: 88

"We Are His Hands"
found in:
CCB: 85

Prayer for the Day / Collect
O God, who makes a path of righteousness and peace in the midst of evil and war, grant us the courage to follow our Savior Jesus as he brings your reign into the midst of the powers that oppose you; through Jesus Christ our Savior. Amen.

OR

We come to join with Jesus as he enters into Jerusalem and makes his stand against evil power and injustice. Help us to not be those who wave their palms but refuse to enter into the sufferings of our Savior. Fill us with courage that we may be true disciples of Jesus. Amen.

Prayer of Confession
Leader: Let us confess to God and before one another our sins and especially the way we speak of our faith so assuredly yet walk the path of Jesus with so much hesitation.
People: We confess to you, O God, and before one another that we have sinned. We are quick to claim our place with Jesus when it enhances our standing with others, but we are loathe to follow him when it costs us friends and popularity. We take the name of Jesus when it makes us look holy and upstanding, but when his values go against the mainstream of society, we hesitate to take a stand. Forgive us and empower us with your Spirit, O God, that we may claim Jesus with our actions as well as with our words. Amen.
Leader: God loves us and is always ready to assist us when we wish to follow the ways of justice, mercy, and humility.

May the Spirit of our God fill you with courage and resolve to follow Jesus.

Prayers of the People (and the Lord's Prayer)
All glory, honor, and power are yours, O God, by right, because you are the Creator and redeemer of all creation. When the powers of evil rise up, you send your Son and your people to stand against them. You are the one who demands justice and mercy for all creation.

(The following paragraph may be used if a separate prayer of confession has not been used.)
We confess to you, O God, and before one another that we have sinned. We are quick to claim our place with Jesus when it enhances our standing with others, but we are loath to follow him when it costs us friends and popularity. We take the name of Jesus when it makes us look holy and upstanding, but when his values go against the mainstream of society, we hesitate to take a stand. Forgive us and empower us with your Spirit, O God, that we may claim Jesus with our actions as well as with our words.

We give you thanks for all the ways you bring your steadfast love and kindness to us and to all creation. We thank you for the opportunities you give us to stand with Jesus on the side of those who are oppressed and misused.

(Other thanksgivings may be offered.)
We pray for your reign to come in its fullness and for us to be faithful servants of you by being faithful caretakers of one another and of all creation.

(Other intercessions may be offered.)
All these things we ask in the name of our Savior Jesus Christ, who taught us to pray together, saying:
Our Father... Amen.

(Or if the Lord's Prayer is not used at this point in the service)

All this we ask in the name of the Blessed and Holy Trinity. Amen.

Maundy Thursday

Exodus 12:1-4 (5-10) 11-14
1 Corinthians 11:23-26
John 13:1-17, 31b-25

Call to Worship

Leader: What shall we return to God for all this bounty to me?

People: We will lift up the cup of salvation and call on the name of our God.

Leader: Let us pay our vows to God in the presence of all the people.

People: We will offer to God a thanksgiving sacrifice.

Leader: Let us call on the name of our God.

People: We will pay our vows to God in the presence of all the people.

OR

Footwashing

Leader: Come into the presence of our Savior.

People: We come to worship and praise the Christ.

Leader: See him kneel before you and wash your feet.

People: We are humbled beyond thought at this.

Leader: See him hand you the basin and towel.

People: We go where he sends us to serve others.

OR

Eucharist

Leader: Come into the presence of our Savior.

People: We come to worship and praise the Christ.

Leader: See him give you his body and blood.

People: We are truly humbled by his sacrifice.
Leader: Now he sends you to give yourself to others.
People: We go where he sends us to give ourselves in the name of the Christ.

Hymns and Sacred Songs
"Go to Dark Gethsemane"
found in:
UMH: 290   CH: 196
H82: 171   LBW: 109
PH: 97   ELW: 347
NCH: 219

"Jesu, Jesu"
found in:
UMH: 432   CH: 600
H82: 602   ELW: 708
PH: 367   CCB: 66
NCH: 498   Renew: 289

"For the Bread Which You Have Broken"
found in:
UMH: 614/615   CH: 411
H82: 340/341   LBW: 200
PH: 508/509   ELW: 494

"Lord, Whose Love Through Humble Service"
found in:
UMH: 582   LBW: 423
H82: 610   ELW: 712
PH: 427   Renew: 286
CH: 461

"Let Us Break Bread Together on Our Knees"
found in:

UMH: 618
H82: 325
PH: 513
AAHH: 686
NNBH: 358

NCH: 330
CH: 425
LBW: 212
ELW: 471
CCB: 46

"Now the Silence"
found in:
UMH: 619
H82: 333
CH: 415

LBW: 205
ELW: 460
Renew: 221

"Here, O My Lord, I See Thee"
found in:
UMH: 623
H82: 318
PH: 520

NCH: 336
CH: 416
LBW: 211

"Lord, Speak to Me"
found in:
UMH: 463
PH: 426

NCH: 531
ELW: 676

"Make Me a Servant"
found in:
CCB: 90

"We Are His Hands"
found in:
CCB: 85

Prayer for the Day / Collect

Footwashing

O God, who has come among us as a servant, grant us the grace to kneel before you in worship and to kneel before others in service; through Jesus Christ our Savior. Amen.

OR

We come, O God, to remember and celebrate that night when Jesus knelt at the feet of his disciples and washed their feet. Help us as we bow before your holiness that we may learn to kneel in service as our Savior Jesus did. Amen.

Eucharist

O God, who has come to give yourself to us, grant us the grace to receive you into our hearts so that we may give ourselves to others: through Jesus Christ our Savior. Amen.

OR

We come, O God, to remember and celebrate the night when Jesus offered himself to his disciples at the Last Supper. Help us as we receive him into ourselves that we may give ourselves in service to others. Amen.

Prayer of Confession

Leader: Let us confess to God and before one another our sins, especially our pride.

People: We confess to you, O God, and before one another that we have sinned. We come to worship our Savior, Jesus, who knelt and washed his disciples' feet and then offered himself to them in that first communion service, and yet we are too proud to follow his example. We are more apt to look down on others than to kneel at their feet. We are more likely to use others than to serve them.

We are more prone to take from others than to give to them. Forgive us our arrogant ways and draw us back to Jesus' side where we may learn to humbly worship you and humbly serve others. Amen.

Leader: Jesus, the humble one, is always ready to receive us. He welcomes us to himself and sends us out to serve others.

Prayers of the People (and the Lord's Prayer)

We come to worship and adore you, O God, for your steadfast love and grace toward us and all your creation. We praise you for your love that gives itself to us over and over again.

(The following paragraph may be used if a separate prayer of confessions has not been used.)

We confess to you, O God, and before one another that we have sinned. We come to worship our Savior, Jesus, who knelt and washed his disciples' feet and then offered himself to them in that first communion service, and yet we are too proud to follow his example. We are more apt to look down on others than to kneel at their feet. We are more likely to use others than to serve them. We are more prone to take from others than to give to them. Forgive us our arrogant ways and draw us back to Jesus' side where we may learn to humbly worship you and humbly serve others.

We give you thanks for all the ways in which you come to us and bring us your gracious love. We thank you for the example of service Jesus has set for us and for his example of sacrificial giving.

(Other thanksgivings may be offered.)

We pray with Jesus for the church and for the world. We pray that we may be faithful as your people, your children, and your image. We pray that our faithful service to the world will draw it closer to you, life, and wholeness.

(Other intercessions may be offered.)
All these things we ask in the name of our Savior Jesus Christ, who taught us to pray together, saying:
Our Father... Amen.

(Or if the Lord's Prayer is not used at this point in the service.)
All this we ask in the name of the Blessed and Holy Trinity. Amen.

Good Friday

Isaiah 52:13—53:12
Hebrews 10:16-25
John 18:1—19:42

Call to Worship
Leader: O my God, I cry by day, but you do not answer;
People: and by night, but I find no rest.
Leader: Yet you are holy, enthroned on the praises of Israel.
People: In you our ancestors trusted.
Leader: Do not be far from me,
People: for trouble is near and there is no one to help.

OR

Leader: Come and stand beneath the cross of Jesus.
People: We come reluctantly because we prefer Easter to Good Friday.
Leader: Come and stand under the love and care of our God.
People: We come in awe that we could be loved like this!
Leader: Come and know that you are God's beloved children.
People: May we share that knowledge with all God's people.

Hymns and Sacred Songs
"O Sacred Head, Now Wounded"
found in:
UMH: 286   NCH: 226
H82: 168/169   CH: 202
PH: 98   LBW: 116/117

AAHH: 250   ELW: 351/352
NNBH: 108   Renew: 235

"What Wondrous Love Is This"
found in:
UMH: 292   CH: 200
H82: 439   LBW: 385
PH: 85   ELW: 666
NCH: 223   Renew: 277

"In the Cross of Christ I Glory"
found in:
UMH: 295   NCH: 193/194
H82: 441/442   LBW: 104
PH: 84   ELW: 324
NNBH: 104

"Ah, Holy Jesus"
found in:
UMH: 289   CH: 210
H82: 158   LBW: 123
PH: 93   ELW: 349
NCH: 218   Renew: 183

"Beneath the Cross of Jesus"
found in:
UMH: 297   NCH: 190
H82: 498   CH: 197
PH: 92   LBW: 107
AAHH: 247   ELW: 338
NNBH: 106

"Were You There"
found in:
UMH: 288   NCH: 229

H82: 172   CH: 198
PH: 102   LBW: 92
AAHH: 254   ELW: 363
NNBH: 109

"Alas! And Did My Saviour Bleed"
found in:
UMH: 294/359   CH: 204
PH: 78   LBW: 98
AAHH: 263/264   ELW: 337
NCH: 199/200

"When I Survey the Wondrous Cross"
found in:
UMH: 298/299   NCH: 224
H82: 474   CH: 195
PH: 100/101   LBW: 482
AAHH: 243   ELW: 803
NNBH: 113   Renew: 236

"O How He Loves You and Me!"
found in:
CCB: 38   Renew: 27

"Only by Grace"
found in:
CCB: 42

Prayer for the Day / Collect

O God, who is love unbounded and eternal, grant us the grace to remember this day with gratitude for your loving kindness to us and to all your creation; through Jesus Christ our Savior. Amen.

OR

We have come this day, O God, to reflect upon the costly sacrifice that love is ever-ready to make for the beloved. Give us grateful hearts to worship you, the giver of love and life. Amen.

Prayer of Confession

Leader: Let us confess to God and before one another our sins and especially our unwillingness to risk ourselves in love.

People: We confess to you, O God, and before one another that we have sinned. We want to be safe. We avoid pain and even being uncomfortable at all costs. We have lost any sense of the common good and are interested only in our own good and that of those closest to us. The whole idea of sacrifice is beyond our comprehension. We are willing to give up little, if anything, for others especially if the others are strangers. Forgive us and call us back to the cross of Jesus so we may see that sacrifice is sometimes the only answer. Make us bold to go forth for you no matter what the cost. Amen.

Leader: God gives all for us. God's love and forgiveness are never ending. Share that with others, even strangers.

Prayers of the People (and the Lord's Prayer)

We praise your name, O God, and glorify you for your ever-giving love for us and for all your creation. You have shown us that there is no limit to your love for us.

(The following paragraph may be used if a separate prayer of confession has not been used.)

We confess to you, O God, and before one another that we have sinned. We want to be safe. We avoid pain and even being uncomfortable at all costs. We have lost any sense of the common good and are interested only in our own good and that of those closest to us. The whole idea of sacrifice is beyond our comprehension. We are willing to give up little, if anything, for others especially if the others are strangers. Forgive us and call us back to the cross of Jesus so we may see that sacrifice is sometimes the only answer. Make us bold to go forth for you no matter what the cost.

We give you thanks for your love and care. We thank you for your church and those within it who have been willing to sacrifice in order for us to come to know you. We thank you for those who have loved us when we have been unlovable and have thus shown us your love.

(Other thanksgivings may be offered.)
We pray for those who are in need. We pray especially for those whose needs have not been met because we have refused to sacrifice our wants to help them in their needs. We pray for ourselves that we might better reflect the Spirit of Jesus and of your love.

(Other intercessions may be offered.)
All these things we ask in the name of our Savior Jesus Christ, who taught us to pray together, saying:
Our Father... Amen.

(Or if the Lord's Prayer is not used at this point in the service)
All this we ask in the name of the Blessed and Holy Trinity. Amen.

Easter Day

Acts 10:34-43
1 Corinthians 15:19-26
John 20:1-18

Call to Worship
Leader: Give thanks to God, for God is good.
People: God's steadfast love endures forever!
Leader: God is our strength and our might.
People: God has become our salvation!
Leader: This day God has acted.
People: Let us rejoice in God's good work!

OR

Leader: Come and hear the good news!
People: What news is good today?
Leader: God has raised Jesus to new life.
People: That certainly is good news for Jesus.
Leader: It is good news for us. Hope has been raised anew.
People: We could use some good news and some hope.
Leader: Nothing is going to defeat the love and purpose of God.
People: Thanks be to God! Jesus and hope are alive forever!

Hymns and Sacred Songs
"Hope of the World"
found in:
UMH: 178   NCH: 46
H82: 472   CH: 538
PH: 360   LBW: 493

"Hymn of Promise"
found in:
UMH: 707   CH: 638
NCH: 433

"My Hope Is Built"
found in:
UMH: 368   NCH: 403
PH: 379   CH: 537
AAHH: 385   LBW: 293/294
NNBH: 274

"O God, Our Help in Ages Past"
found in:
UMH: 368   NCH: 25
H82: 680   CH: 67
AAHH: 170   LBW: 320
NNBH: 46

"O Day of Peace that Dimly Shines"
found in:
UMH: 729   PH: 450
H82: 597   CH: 711

"Sing Unto the Lord a New Song"
found in:
CCB: 16

"Your Loving Kindness Is Better than Life"
CCB: 26

Prayer for the Day / Collect
O God, who raised Jesus from death and gave the disciples
hope once again, grant that we may find in his resurrection

our hope for eternal life now and forever; through Jesus Christ our Savior. Amen.

OR

We have come to rejoice and praise you, O God, for the wonder of the resurrection. We praise your name as you bring Jesus and all your people to new life and new hope. So fill us with the joy of your Spirit that we may spread the good news throughout the land. Amen.

Prayer of Confession
Leader: Let us confess to God and before one another our sins and especially our lack of faith which leads us to a life without hope.
People: We confess to you, O God, and before one another that we have sinned. We have failed to look to you for hope. We have been overwhelmed by the negative all around us. Without the hope that is grounded in you we have had nothing to share with the world. Forgive us and renew in us the good news of Easter that we may find our hope renewed and share it with all the world. Amen.
Leader: God comes to bring life, joy, and hope to all creation. God comes to claim us and renew us that we may be signs of hope for others. Rejoice in God's love and grace for you and for all creation.

Prayers of the People (and the Lord's Prayer)
We worship and adore you, O God, for the wonder of your power. You created all that is and when we rejected your life within us, you came to renew and restore us.

(The following paragraph may be used if a separate prayer of confession has not been used.)

We confess to you, O God, and before one another that we have sinned. We have failed to look to you for hope. We have been overwhelmed by the negative all around us. Without the hope that is grounded in you we have had nothing to share with the world. Forgive us and renew in us the good news of Easter that we may find our hope renewed and share it with all the world.

We give you thanks for all the ways you express your love for us. We thank you for the beauty of the world and the joy of sharing love with one another. We thank you for hope and lives that have found new joy and fulfillment in your grace.

(Other thanksgivings may be offered.)
We pray for one another in our need and for all people anywhere who have lost hope. As you move among your children bringing new life, grant that we may be your joyful people sharing the good news of hope that is grounded in you.

(Other intercessions may be offered.)
All these things we ask in the name of our Savior Jesus Christ, who taught us to pray together, saying:
Our Father... Amen.

(Or if the Lord's Prayer is not used at this point in the service)
All this we ask in the name of the Blessed and Holy Trinity. Amen.

Easter 2

Acts 5:27-32
Revelation 1:4-8
John 20:19-31

Call to Worship
Leader: Praise God! Praise God in the sanctuary!
People: Praise God for mighty deeds!
Leader: Praise God with trumpet sound!
People: Praise God with lute and harp!
Leader: Let everything that breathes praise God!
People: Praise God for ever and ever.

OR

Leader: Come and worship God with body, mind, and Spirit.
People: I come to worship, but I have questions about God.
Leader: God welcomes you and your questions.
People: Isn't faith opposed to questions?
Leader: It actually takes faith to ask God questions.
People: Then I will come and offer myself and my questions.

Hymns and Sacred Songs
"When Our Confidence Is Shaken"
found in:
UMH: 505 CH: 534

"Faith, While Trees Are Still in Blossom"
found in:
UMH: 508 CH: 535

"Thy Word Is a Lamp"
found in:
UMH: 601   CH: 326

"Open My Eyes, that I May See"
found in:
UMH: 454   NNBH: 218
PH: 324   CH: 586

"Be Thou My Vision"
found in:
UMH: 451   NCH: 451
H82: 488   CH: 595
PH: 339

"Unity"
found in:
CCB: 59

"Open Our Eyes, Lord"
found in:
CCB: 77

Prayer for the Day / Collect
O God, who created us with reason and intellect, grant that we may use the gifts you have presented to us not to destroy faith and community but to strengthen it; through Jesus Christ our Savior. Amen.

OR

We come to worship and adore our Creator and redeemer. You have made us in your image and imparted to us a wisdom that reflects, in a small measure, your own. As we praise you and listen for your voice, so fill us with your Spirit that we may properly discern how you desire to be at work in, among, and through us. Amen.

Prayer of Confession
Leader: Let us confess to God and before one another our sins and especially our quickness to move to doubt or faith without the hard work of discernment.

People: We confess to you, O God, and before one another that we have sinned. We want things to be clear and simple. We want quick answers that comfort us and don't ask too much of us. We are glad to have someone tell us what to think as long as we already think that way. We don't want to be challenged, and we don't want to have to work out our salvation with fear and trembling. Forgive us and renew your Spirit within us that we may truly seek you and your truth. Amen.

Leader: God knows us and knows that seeking what is true and right is hard work. God grants us his Spirit so that we are able to take on the task of discernment. God invites you to drink once again from the waters of life and to be renewed in the power of the Spirit for the work ahead of you.

Prayers of the People (and the Lord's Prayer)
We worship and praise your name, O God, for the glory of your creative power. Your wisdom and knowledge are beyond our understanding and yet you have granted us the ability to share in the power of thought and reason.

(The following paragraph may be used if a separate prayer of confession has not been used.)
We confess to you, O God, and before one another that we have sinned. We want things to be clear and simple. We want quick answers that comfort us and don't ask too much of us. We are glad to have someone tell us what to think as long as we already think that way. We don't want to be challenged,

and we don't want to have to work out our salvation with fear and trembling. Forgive us and renew your Spirit within us that we may truly seek you and your truth.

We give you thanks for the glories of nature and for the way you have made us so that we can comprehend and appreciate those glories. We thank you for the ability to reason and to think and most of all for the ability to be open to your presence in creation and in our lives.

(Other thanksgivings may be offered.)
We offer into your love those who are in need of healing in mind, body, or Spirit. We pray for those who are struggling with their faith and dealing with questions about what they really believe. We pray that we may be a community of compassion, openness, and safety for those who are in the midst of their search for truth.

(Other intercessions may be offered.)
All these things we ask in the name of our Savior Jesus Christ, who taught us to pray together, saying:
Our Father... Amen.

(Or if the Lord's Prayer is not used at this point in the service)
All this we ask in the name of the Blessed and Holy Trinity. Amen.

Easter 3

Acts 9:1-6 (7-20)
Revelation 5:11-14
John 21:1-19

Call to Worship
Leader: O God, you brought up my soul from death.
People: You restored my life from those who have died.
Leader: Sing praise to God, you faithful ones.
People: We give thanks to God's holy name.
Leader: God has turned our mourning into dancing.
People: We will give thanks to God forever.

OR

Leader: Come into the presence of the Holy One.
People: It scares me to come before God.
Leader: It is right and good to fear the presence of God.
People: Should I fear because God is angry?
Leader: No. You should fear because God is love. You should fear because God wants us to grow and change.
People: It is scary to change, but I can with God's help.

Hymns and Sacred Songs
"Take My Hand, Precious Lord"
found in:
NNBH: 305

"Lord, Take My Hand and Lead Me"
found in:
LBW: 333

"Lead Me, Lord"
found in:
UMH: 473
AAHH: 145
NNBH: 341

CH: 593
Renew: 175

"Have Thine Own Way, Lord"
found in:
UMH: 382
AAHH: 449

NNBH: 206
CH: 588

"Jesus Calls Us"
found in:
UMH: 398
H82: 549/550
NNBH: 183

NCH: 171/172
CH: 337
LBW: 494

"Close to Thee"
found in:
UMH: 407
AAHH: 552/553

NNBH: 317

"Dear Lord, Lead Me Day by Day"
found in:
UMH: 411

"Change My Heart, O God"
found in:
CCB: 56

Renew: 143

"Create in Me a Clean Heart"
found in:
CCB: 54

Renew: 181/182

Prayer for the Day / Collect

O God, who desires to draw us with cords of love, grant us the grace to allow you to lead us by the hand and to be open to those you send to lead us to you; through Jesus Christ our Savior. Amen.

OR

We come to worship you, our God and our guide. We sing your praises and we look to you for the direction our lives need. We lift our hands in praise so that we can take your hand that leads us. Receive our praises and help us to walk with you in humility. Amen.

Prayer of Confession

Leader: Let us confess to God and before one another our sins and especially our unwillingness to be led by you or by anyone.

People: We confess to you, O God, and before one another that we have sinned. We are a strong-willed and stubborn people who often insist that things must be done our way. We want to be leaders, and we chafe at the idea that we may have to be followers. We even resist your efforts to lead us to a life of joy and peace. Forgive our foolishness and grant that by the power of your Spirit we may learn to quietly take your hand and follow where you lead. Amen.

Leader: God desires nothing more than our good. Whenever we are willing to let go of the reins and let God lead, God will take us where we need to go. Follow God with confidence and joy.

Prayers of the People (and the Lord's Prayer)

We glorify your name, O God, for you are the one who loves us and cares for us more deeply than we could ever understand. You are the one who leads us to a life full of joy and peace.

(The following paragraph may be used if a separate prayer of confession has not been used.)
We confess to you, O God, and before one another that we have sinned. We are a strong-willed and stubborn people who often insist that things must be done our way. We want to be leaders, and we chafe at the idea that we may have to be followers. We even resist your efforts to lead us to a life of joy and peace. Forgive our foolishness and grant that by the power of your Spirit we may learn to quietly take your hand and follow where you lead.

We give you thanks for all the ways you have given us direction. We thank you for those who had a clearer view or who heard more precisely or who felt more deeply what you would have us to do to grow in your love, and who then faithfully shared that good news with us.

(Other thanksgivings may be offered.)
We pray for ourselves and for all, anywhere, who need to feel your loving hand leading them.

(Other intercessions may be offered.)
All these things we ask in the name of our Savior Jesus Christ, who taught us to pray together, saying:
Our Father... Amen.

(Or if the Lord's Prayer is not used at this point in the service)
All this we ask in the name of the Blessed and Holy Trinity. Amen.

Easter 4

Acts 9:36-43
Revelation 7:9-17
John 10:22-30

Call to Worship
Leader: God is our shepherd.
People: We have no other needs.
Leader: Even though I walk through the darkest valley,
People: I will fear no evil.
Leader: Surely goodness and mercy shall follow us always.
People: We shall dwell in the house of God for ever.

OR

Leader: Fear not, God is with us!
People: But the world is a scary place.
Leader: The world is scary, but God is with us.
People: The evil of the world overwhelms me.
Leader: But it doesn't overwhelm God.
People: We will trust in God and we will overcome.

Hymns and Sacred Songs
"Be Still, My Soul"
found in:

UMH: 534	NCH: 488
AAHH: 135	CH: 566
NNBH: 263	

"Give to the Winds Thy Fears"
found in:

UMH: 129	PH: 286

"We Shall Overcome"
found in:
UMH: 533   NCH: 570
AAHH: 542   CH: 630
NNBH: 501

"Turn Your Eyes Upon Jesus"
found in:
UMH: 349   NNBH: 195

"Out of the Depths I Cry to You"
found in:
UMH: 515   NCH: 483
H82: 666   CH: 510
PH: 240   LBW: 295

"Hope of the World"
found in:
UMH: 178   NCH: 46
H82: 472   CH: 538
PH: 360   LBW: 493

"Leaning on the Everlasting Arms"
found in:
UMH: 133   NCH: 471
AAHH: 371   CH: 560
NNBH: 262

"O Mary, Don't You Weep"
found in:
UMH: 134

"All I Need Is You"
found in:
CCB: 100

"The Steadfast Love of the Lord"
found in:
CCB: 28   Renew: 23

Prayer for the Day / Collect

O God, who created us to live without fear in your love, grant us the grace to truly trust in your compassion and care that we may not fear anything in this life or the life to come; through Jesus Christ our Savior. Amen.

OR

We have come to this time of worship, O God, to offer our praise and thanksgiving to you. We come in awe of your greatness, and you offer to receive us in love and compassion. Help us not to fear that which is around us, since we are always held in your gracious hand. Amen.

Prayer of Confession

Leader: Let us confess to God and before one another our sins and especially the way we let our fears determine our actions.

People: We confess to you, O God, and before one another that we have sinned. We have focused our eyes on those things around us and in our fear of them, we have forsaken your path. We fear the evil things around us. We fear the thought of being poor or naked or homeless. We fear becoming ill and dying. We fear being embarrassed or ridiculed. We fear life. Forgive us and by the power of your Spirit fill us with such faith in you that we will never fear. Amen.

Leader: God's love and grace is sufficient for us. God loves us perfectly and perfect love casts out fear. May the grace of God grow in your hearts as you live bravely in the presence and power of God.

Prayers of the People (and the Lord's Prayer)
We worship you, our God and our shepherd, for you are the one who is and was and is to come. You are the eternal one who holds us safely in your own hand.

(The following paragraph may be used if a separate prayer of confession has not been used.)
We confess to you, O God, and before one another that we have sinned. We have focused our eyes on those things around us and in our fear of them, we have forsaken your path. We fear the evil things around us. We fear the thought of being poor or naked or homeless. We fear becoming ill and dying. We fear being embarrassed or ridiculed. We fear life. Forgive us and by the power of your Spirit fill us with such faith in you that we will never fear.

We give you thanks for all the times we have been aware of your presence in our midst. We give you thanks for all the times you have walked with us and carried us and we were unaware of your being there. We thank you for those you have sent to nurture and assist us in the difficult times of life. Most of all we thank you for Jesus, who came to share the good news with us that we do not need to fear, for you are always with us and for us.

(Other thanksgivings may be offered.)
We pray for those who live in fear. We know that life is hard for many who are hungry, homeless, and lost. We pray that as you encircle them with your love and care, you would enable us to be a brave presence helping them to trust you and to give up their fears.

(Other intercessions may be offered.)
All these things we ask in the name of our Savior Jesus Christ, who taught us to pray together, saying:
Our Father... Amen.

(Or if the Lord's Prayer is not used at this point in the service)

All this we ask in the name of the Blessed and Holy Trinity. Amen.

Easter 5

Acts 11:1-18
Revelation 21:1-6
John 13:31-35

Call to Worship
Leader: Praise God from the heavens!
People: Praise God from the heights!
Leader: Let all creation praise our God!
People: For God is the Creator of all!
Leader: Young and old, men and women, praise God!
People: Praise God, whose glory is above earth and heaven!

OR

Leader: Come and hear the command of our Savior.
People: Speak, Jesus; your servants are listening.
Leader: "Love one another."
People: We try to like each other.
Leader: "Love one another, as I have loved you."
People: We are your disciples; we will obey.

Hymns and Sacred Songs
"In Christ There Is No East or West"
found in:

UMH: 548	NNBH: 289
H82: 529	NCH: 394/395
PH: 439/440	CH: 687
AAHH: 398/399	LBW: 259

"Help Us Accept Each Other"
found in:

UMH: 560 NCH: 388
PH: 358 CH: 487

"Jesus, United by Thy Grace"
found in:
UMH: 561

"Father, We Thank You"
found in:
UMH: 563 H82: 302/303

"Blest Be the Dear Uniting Love"
found in:
UMH: 566

"All Creatures of Our God and King"
found in:
UMH: 62 NCH: 17
H82: 400 CH: 22
PH: 455 LBW: 527
AAHH: 147 Renew: 47
NNBH: 33

"All People that on Earth Do Dwell"
found in:
UMH: 75 NCH: 7
H82: 377/378 CH: 18
PH: 220/221 LBW: 245
NNBH: 36

"God, Whose Love Is Reigning O'er Us"
found in:
UMH: 100

"Shine, Jesus, Shine"
found in:
CCB: 81   Renew: 247

"I Am Loved"
found in:
CCB: 80

Prayer for the Day / Collect

O God, who created us to live in peace and harmony with you and with one another, grant us the grace to see you as our loving Creator and to see others as your beloved children; through Jesus Christ our Savior. Amen.

OR

We have gathered to worship you, our Creator and redeemer God, who has made us to live in communion with you and in peace with all your children. As we worship you and listen for your voice, help us not to forget that you call us to love one another as much as you call us to love you. So fill us with your loving Spirit that we will be filled with love for all creation. Amen.

Prayer of Confession

Leader: Let us confess to God and before one another our sins and especially the way we divide people into groups and judge them by whether they are like us or not.
People: We confess to you, O God, and before one another that we have sinned. You have created us for love, and yet we live most of our lives unaware of your presence. You give us every good and perfect gift, and we take and use them without giving a thought to the giver. You created us all as your children, but we act like you only

love us and those just like us. Forgive us for being so foolish and self-centered. Open our hearts with the power of your Spirit that we may love you more fully and love others as we love ourselves. Amen.

Leader: God does love us, each and every one. Receive the love and forgiveness of our God and remember that the same Spirit that was in Christ Jesus is now in you. Let that Spirit love the world through you.

Prayers of the People (and the Lord's Prayer)

All glory and praise is yours by right, O God, for you are the Creator of all that is and was and will be. All life comes from your life. All love comes from your love.

(The following paragraph may be used if a separate prayer of confession has not been used.)

We confess to you, O God, and before one another that we have sinned. You have created us for love, and yet we live most of our lives unaware of your presence. You give us every good and perfect gift, and we take and use them without giving a thought to the giver. You created us all as your children, but we act like you only love us and those just like us. Forgive us for being so foolish and self-centered. Open our hearts with the power of your Spirit that we may love you more fully and love others as we love ourselves.

We give you thanks for all the ways your love has touched our lives. We give you thanks that your love has made us and given us life. We thank you for the joy of creation and for the joy of living in communion with you and in community with your children. We thank you for Jesus who showed us how to love you and one another.

(Other thanksgivings may be offered.)

We pray to you for our sisters and brothers, wherever they may live. We pray that as you draw them closer to you, they will find themselves drawn closer to others. We pray this for ourselves, as well.

(Other intercessions may be offered.)
All these things we ask in the name of our Savior Jesus Christ, who taught us to pray together, saying:
Our Father... Amen.

(Or if the Lord's Prayer is not used at this point in the service)
All this we ask in the name of the Blessed and Holy Trinity. Amen.

Easter 6

Acts 16:9-15
Revelation 21:10, 22—22:5
John 14:23-29

Call to Worship
Leader: May God be gracious to us and bless us.
People: Let the peoples praise you, O God.
Leader: Let the nations be glad and sing for joy,
People: for God judges the peoples with equity.
Leader: May God continue to bless us.
People: Let all the ends of the earth revere God.

OR

Leader: God comes among us in glory.
People: God's glory fills the earth.
Leader: God comes among us with holiness.
People: God calls us to holiness as well.
Leader: We worship the God who comes among us.
People: We join in the holy life of our God.

Hymns and Sacred Songs
"All Glory, Laud, and Honor"
found in:
UMH: 280   NNBH: 102
H82: 154/155   NCH: 216/217
PH: 88   CH: 192
AAHH: 226   LBW: 108

"Crown Him with Many Crowns"
found in:
UMH: 327   NNBH: 125

H82: 494   NCH: 301
PH: 151   CH: 234
AAHH: 288   LBW: 170

"Glorious Things of Thee Are Spoken"
found in:
UMH: 731   NCH: 307
H82: 522/523   CH: 709
PH: 446   LBW: 358
NNBH: 426

"Holy God, We Praise Thy Name"
found in:
UMH: 79   NNBH: 13
H82: 366   NCH: 276
PH: 460   LBW: 535

Prayer for the Day / Collect
O God, who is the Holy One, grant us the grace to live in holiness as you come among us in this world; through Jesus Christ our Savior. Amen.

OR

We come to worship you, the Holy One, and to welcome you into our presence. You come among us and there is no need for a temple. You are the true presence of holiness. Help us to worship you and join you in truth. Amen.

Prayer of Confession
Leader: Let us confess to God and before one another our sins and especially our inclination to worship things instead of you.
People: We confess to you, O God, and before one another that we have sinned. We have erected temples and we

139

have worshiped at false altars. We have raised up wealth, fame, and greed as things to be adored. We have placed things above you and above one another. We have sacrificed each other and our own souls to gain possessions. Forgive us and call us back to worship you, the Holy One, who knows no falsehood. By the power of your Spirit let us live in truth and holiness with you. Amen.

Leader: God knows how easily we are pulled away. God knows what we are made of. God loves us and invites us back home.

Prayers of the People (and the Lord's Prayer)

We praise and adore you, O God, for all the glory and holiness that is yours. You are the one whose actions and intentions are one.

(The following paragraph may be used if a separate prayer of confession has not been used.)

We confess to you, O God, and before one another that we have sinned. We have erected temples and we have worshiped at false altars. We have raised up wealth, fame, and greed as things to be adored. We have placed things above you and above one another. We have sacrificed each other and our own souls to gain possessions. Forgive us and call us back to worship you, the Holy One, who knows no falsehood. By the power of your Spirit let us live in truth and holiness with you.

We thank you for all the ways your steadfast love is shown to us. We thank you for being with us in good times and bad. We thank you for the times we are aware of your presence and for the times you are with us and we are oblivious.

(Other thanksgivings may be offered.)

We pray for one another in our need to center our lives in you, so that in whatever life brings us we will find wholeness and blessing. We pray that as we open ourselves to you, we will be able to open ourselves more fully to one another.

(Other intercessions may be offered.)
All these things we ask in the name of our Savior Jesus Christ, who taught us to pray together, saying:
Our Father... Amen.

(Or if the Lord's Prayer is not used at this point in the service)
All this we ask in the name of the Blessed and Holy Trinity. Amen.

Ascension of Our Lord / Easter 7

Acts 1:1-11
Ephesians 1:15-23
Luke 24:44-53

Call to Worship
Leader: God reigns! Let the earth rejoice.
People: The heavens proclaim God's righteousness;
Leader: all the peoples behold God's glory.
People: Zion hears and is glad.
Leader: God loves those who hate evil;
People: God guards the lives of the faithful.

OR

Leader: Come and worship God with an open heart.
People: If we open our hearts, God will know who we are.
Leader: God already knows you and loves you still.
People: We come and open our hearts and lives to God.
Leader: This is the community of faith you belong to as well.
People: We will be truthful to our sisters and brothers.

Hymns and Sacred Songs
"Holy Spirit, Truth Divine"
found in:
UMH: 465   CH: 241
PH: 321   LBW: 257
NCH: 63

"I Want a Principle Within"
found in:
UMH: 410

"How Shall They Hear the Word of God"
found in:
UMH: 649

"Take My Life, and Let It Be"
found in:
UMH: 399	NCH: 448
H82: 707	CH: 609
PH: 391	LBW: 406
NNBH: 213	Renew: 150

"Only Trust Him"
found in:
UMH: 337	NNBH: 193
AAHH: 369	

"O Come and Dwell in Me"
found in:
UMH: 388

"A Charge to Keep I Have"
found in:
UMH: 413	NNBH: 436
AAHH: 467/468	

"O Young and Fearless Prophet"
found in:
UMH: 444	CH: 669

"Dear Jesus, in Whose Life I See"
found in:

UMH: 468

"Refiner's Fire"
found in:
CCB: 79

"Humble Yourself in the Sight of the Lord"
found in:
CCB: 72   Renew: 188

Prayer for the Day / Collect
O God, who is truth itself, grant us the grace and courage to
be honest and open to you about ourselves and to not deceive
others about who we are that all may know they can trust our
witness through Jesus Christ our Savior. Amen.

OR

We come to worship you, O God, who dwells in truth eternal. In you there is no wavering or straying from the truth.
You act out with integrity who you are, and you invite us to
do the same. So fill us with your Spirit that only the truth will
dwell in us, and we will be faithful witnesses of Jesus, our
Savior. Amen.

Prayer of Confession
Leader: Let us confess to God and before one another our
sins and especially the way we avoid the hard work of truth-
telling.
**People: We confess to you, O God, and before one an-
other that we have sinned. We have lived in deceit and
falsehood. Sometimes we have boldly and knowingly lied
about ourselves and about others. Sometimes we have
"shaded" the truth, and we do it so often we usually are
not even aware of it. Sometimes when we hear lies being**

told we do not stand up for the truth. In all these things we deny you. We place a barrier in the lives of others who learn not to trust us, and so they do not believe what we tell them about you. Forgive us and empower us with your Spirit for truth and for witness. Amen.

Leader: God delights in the truth and welcomes you into it. God loves us enough to allow us to be truthful with and about ourselves. Know that God is not deceived. God knows who we are and loves us unconditionally.

Prayers of the People (and the Lord's Prayer)

We worship and adore you, O God, for you are the very essence of truth. In you there is no shadow or turning from the truth. Because you are love, you do not need to hide yourself from us or deceive yourself about who we are. Your love is strong because there is not falsehood in your relationship with creation.

(The following paragraph may be used if a separate prayer of confession has not been used.)

We confess to you, O God, and before one another that we have sinned. We have lived in deceit and falsehood. Sometimes we have boldly and knowingly lied about ourselves and about others. Sometimes we have "shaded" the truth, and we do it so often we usually are not even aware of it. Sometimes when we hear lies being told we do not stand up for the truth. In all these things we deny you. We place a barrier in the lives of others who learn not to trust us, and so they do not believe what we tell them about you. Forgive us and empower us with your Spirit for truth and for witness.

We give you thanks for the great love with which you hold us and that enables us to live before you in honesty and truth. We thank you for those who have lived with integrity before us so that we have come to accept their testimony about you and your love.

(Other thanksgivings may be offered.)
We pray for ourselves and for others who have allowed fear
to overrule love and honesty. We pray for the dispelling of
that spirit of fear so that we might live with joy and honesty
before your face.

(Other intercessions may be offered.)
All these things we ask in the name of our Savior Jesus
Christ, who taught us to pray together, saying:
Our Father... Amen.

*(Or if the Lord's Prayer is not used at this point in the ser-
vice)*
All this we ask in the name of the Blessed and Holy Trinity.
Amen.

Pentecost Sunday

Acts 2:1-21
Romans 8:14-17
John 14:8-17 (25-27)

Call to Worship
Leader: How manifold are the works of God!
People: In wisdom, God has made them all.
Leader: The earth is full of God's creatures.
People: They look to God to feed them in due season.
Leader: God will pour out the Spirit on all his daughters and sons.
People: We shall see visions and dream dreams.

OR

Leader: God calls us to come and receive the Holy Spirit.
People: With joy we come to receive God's gift.
Leader: This is the same Spirit that was in Jesus, the servant.
People: By the power of Jesus' Spirit we will serve as he did.
Leader: God desires for all the world to serve and be redeemed.
People: We will go where God sends us and do as God asks.

Hymns and Sacred Songs
(I have included several hymns/songs that are appropriate for Pentecost and reflect different cultures. This is a small number of hymns and can be supplemented by others in your hymnal.)

"Many Gifts, One Spirit"
found in:
UMH: 114   NCH: 177

"Spirit of God, Descend Upon My Heart"
found in:
UMH: 500   NCH: 290
PH: 326   CH: 265
AAHH: 312   LBW: 486

"Spirit of the Living God"
found in:
UMH: 393   NCH: 283
PH: 323   CH: 259
AAHH: 320   Renew: 90
NNBH: 133

"Filled with the Spirit's Power"
found in:
UMH: 537   LBW: 160
NCH: 266

"Cantemos al Senor" ("Let's Sing unto the Lord")
found in:
UMH: 149   CH: 60
NCH: 39   Renew: 11

"Daw-Kee, Aim Daw-Tsi-Taw" ("Great Spirit, Now I Pray")
found in:
UMH: 330

"Heleluyan" ("Alleluia")
found in:

UMH: 78   Renew: 137
PH: 595

"*Jaya Ho*" ("Victory Hymn")
found in:
UMH: 478

"Sanctuary"
found in:
CCB: 87   Renew: 185

"People Need the Lord"
found in:
CCB: 52

"*Je Louerai l'Eternel*" ("Praise, I Will Praise You, Lord")
found in:
Renew: 76

Prayer for the Day / Collect
O God, whose Spirit hovered over the waters and creation and breathed into that first human, grant us the grace and the courage to go forth in the power of your Spirit and claim your creation for your glory; through Jesus Christ our Savior. Amen.

OR

We have come to worship you, the Creator and redeemer of creation. By your Spirit we were created, by your Spirit we have been empowered, and by your Spirit your creation will be claimed for you and for your reign. So fill us with that Spirit that we will be bold in making this world the place where you reign; through Jesus Christ our Savior. Amen.

149

Prayer of Confession

Leader: Let us confess to God and before one another our sins and especially the way we shirk our opportunities to reach out in the power of your Spirit and claim this world for you.

People: We confess to you, O God, and before one another that we have sinned. We are happy and quick to be your people who are filled with your Spirit and yet we are reluctant to use the power of your Spirit to make the world into the realm you desire it to become. We hesitate to speak out against injustice, we are slow to speak words of care and love, and we allow the world to go on its way to destruction without giving even a thought. Forgive us our hard-heartedness and reawaken within us your call to be the body of Christ in this world so that we allow the Spirit to work freely within us and through us for your glory and purposes. Amen.

Leader: God desires to claim all creation — even us, God's wayward and unfaithful children. God loves us all and claims us all. Know God's forgiveness and share it with those around us.

Prayers of the People (and the Lord's Prayer)

We worship you and adore you, O God, who created the world for communion with yourself and out of the depths of your love.

(The following paragraph may be used if a separate prayer of confession has not been used.)

We confess to you, O God, and before one another that we have sinned. We are happy and quick to be your people who are filled with your Spirit, and yet we are reluctant to use the power of your Spirit to make the world into the realm you desire it to become. We hesitate to speak out against injustice, we are slow to speak words of care and love, and we allow the world to go on its way to destruction without giving even a thought. Forgive us our hard-heartedness and reawaken within us your call to be the body of Christ in this world so that we allow the Spirit to work freely within us and through us for your glory and purposes.

We give you thanks for all the signs that you love us and all your creation. We thank you for the beauty in the world and for the constant presence of your Spirit among and within us. We thank you for the privilege of being your Spirit-bearers and of being part of your good news for all creation.

(Other thanksgivings may be offered.)
We pray to you for one another's needs and for those, anywhere, who are struggling in this life. We know that many suffer physically, spiritually, and mentally. We know that many find relationships to be difficult and in need of healing. We live in a broken world that you are ever healing. Make us instruments of that healing so that your joy and purpose may be fulfilled.

(Other intercessions may be offered.)
All these things we ask in the name of our Savior Jesus Christ, who taught us to pray together, saying:
Our Father... Amen.

(Or if the Lord's Prayer is not used at this point in the service)
All this we ask in the name of the Blessed and Holy Trinity. Amen.

Holy Trinity Sunday

Proverbs 8:1-4, 22-31
Romans 5:1-5
John 16:12-15

Call to Worship
Leader: O God, our Sovereign, how majestic is your name.
People: Your glory, O God, is above the heavens.
Leader: We look at the universe you have created,
People: and we are in awe that you care for us.
Leader: You have made us only a little lower than yourself,
People: and you have committed your creation to us.

OR

Leader: God calls us into worship and into life.
People: We have come to sing God's praises.
Leader: God lives not only in our praises but in our troubles.
People: It is not easy to see God in our problems.
Leader: If we look with faith, we see God incarnate in all of our lives.
People: We will look for God and follow Jesus every day.

Hymns and Songs
"I Want Jesus to Walk with Me"

UMH 521	NNBH 500
PH 363	NCH 490
AAHH 563	CH 627

"Saranam, Saranam"

UMH 523	CCB 73

"What a Friend We Have in Jesus"
UMH 526   NCH 506
PH 403   CH 585
AAHH 430/431   LBW 439
NNBH 61

"Nearer, My God, to Thee"
UMH 528   NCH 606
AAHH 163   CH 577
NNBH 314

"Be Still, My Soul"
UMH 534   NCH 488
AAHH 135   CH 566
NNBH 263

"I Need Thee Every Hour"
UMH 397   NCH 517
AAHH 451   CH 578
NNBH 303

"Jesus Calls Us"
UMH 398   NCH 171/172
H82 549/550   CH 337
NNBH 183   LBW 494

"Great Is Thy Faithfulness"
UMH 140   NCH 423
AAHH 158   CH 86
NNBH 45   Renew 249

"Through It All"
CCB 61

"Something Beautiful"
CCB 84

Prayer for the Day/Collect
O God, you know that we are but creatures of the earth who know pain and suffering, grant us the grace to endure our hardships that you may work in us to redeem them for our salvation; through Jesus Christ our Savior. Amen.

OR

O God who is truth, grant us the courage to live truthfully before you, ourselves, and one another; through Jesus Christ our Savior. Amen.

Prayer of Confession
Leader: Let us confess to God and before one another our sins and especially the way we deny that suffering is a part of life and the way we blame people for their own suffering.
People: We confess to you, O God, and before one another that we have sinned. We want life to be all smiles and good times. We want everything to be effortless and easy. When things don't go as we had hoped we complain that life is not fair to us because we do not deserve to have troubles. When these same things happen to others outside our little circle, we blame them for bringing on their own problems. We avoid those opportunities to grow by dealing with our setbacks in mature ways. We avoid those opportunities to grow in compassion for others who suffer. Forgive us and empower us with your Spirit that we may walk with Jesus through our difficulties and find new life as he did. Empower us to walk with others so they may find comfort and meaning in their own sufferings. Amen.

Leader: God, our loving parent, wants us to grow into the beautiful adult children we were created to become. God grants us forgiveness and the Spirit of Jesus to empower us and enable us to grow into the very likeness of our Savior.

Prayers of the People

You, O God, have created the world to be a place for your children to grow and mature. You have made this world to be a good place. You have filled it with beauty and with your own presence.

(The following paragraph may be used if a separate prayer of confessions has not been used.)

We confess to you, O God, and before one another that we have sinned. We want life to be all smiles and good times. We want everything to be effortless and easy. When things don't go as we had hoped we complain that life is not fair to us because we do not deserve to have troubles. When these same things happen to others outside our little circle, we blame them for bringing on their own problems. We avoid those opportunities to grow by dealing with our setbacks in mature ways. We avoid those opportunities to grow in compassion for others who suffer. Forgive us and empower us with your Spirit that we may walk with Jesus through our difficulties and find new life as he did. Empower us to walk with others so they may find comfort and meaning in their own sufferings.

We give you thanks for all the ways we find your love and grace surrounding us. We thank you for the good earth that provides not only for our needs but delights our senses with its beauty. We thank you for the Spirit of Jesus that guides us and helps us deal with difficulties that enter our lives. We thank you for the ability to reason and to see beyond the moment. We thank you that you created us to learn and to grow in spirit and mind as well as body.

155

(Other thanksgivings may be offered.)
We pray for each other in our need and for all who suffer this day. We pray that where it is possible to overcome that suffering, healing, wholeness, and truth will prevail. Where suffering will not abate, we pray for comfort, strength, and the ability to not let it destroy the spirit within.

(Other intercessions may be offered.)
All these things we ask in the name of our Savior Jesus Christ, who taught us to pray together, saying:
Our Father ... Amen.

(Or if the Our Father is not used at this point in the service)
All this we ask in the name of the Blessed and Holy Trinity. Amen.

Proper 4
Pentecost 2
Ordinary Time 9

1 Kings 18:20-21 (22-29) 30-39
Galatians 1:1-12
Luke 7:1-10

Call to Worship
Leader: O sing to God a new song;
People: sing to God, all the earth.
Leader: Sing to God, bless God's name;
People: tell of God's salvation from day to day.
Leader: Declare God's glory among the nations,
People: God's marvelous works among all the peoples.

OR

Leader: Come and worship the God who loves us.
People: We offer our praise to the God who is love.
Leader: Our God is the one who comes to dwell with us.
People: We rejoice in the loving presence of our God.
Leader: Our God comes to bring us wholeness and life.
People: Our life and salvation are in our God.

Hymns and Sacred Songs
"Prayer Is the Soul's Sincere Desire"
found in:
UMH: 492   NCH: 508

"Sweet Hour of Prayer"
found in:

UMH: 498   NCH: 505
AAHH: 442   CH: 570
NNBH: 332

"Stand By Me"
found in:
UMH: 512   CH: 629
NNBH: 318

"Out of the Depths I Cry to You"
found in:
UMH: 513   CH: 510
H82: 666   LBW: 295
PH: 240   ELW: 600
NCH: 483

"Come, Ye Disconsolate"
found in:
UMH: 510   CH: 502
AAHH: 421   ELW: 607
NNBH: 264

"The Old Rugged Cross"
found in:
UMH: 504   NCH: 195
AAHH: 244   CH: 548
NNBH: 105

"Leaning on the Everlasting Arms"
found in:
UMH: 133   NCH: 471
AAHH: 371   CH: 560
NNBH: 262   ELW: 774

"God Will Take Care of You"
found in:
UMH: 130   NNBH: 52
AAHH: 137   NCH: 460

"Sweet, Sweet Spirit"
found in:
CCB: 7   NNBH: 127
UMH: 334   NCH: 293
AAHH: 326   CH: 261

"I Will Call Upon the Lord"
found in:
CCB: 9   Renew: 15

Prayer for the Day / Collect

O God, who draws near to listen to your children, give us the faith to trust that you truly care for us and desire us to have life and wholeness in you; through Jesus Christ our Savior. Amen.

OR

We come to worship you, O God, for you are the one who comes to us. In love and care you open your heart to our needs. You desire our good and our salvation and so we praise your holy name. Amen.

Prayer of Confession

Leader: Let us confess to God and before one another our sins and especially the way we doubt your care for us.
People: We confess to you, O God, and before one another that we have sinned. You created us out of love and you have become one of us so that we may find salvation in you, and yet we act and talk as if you do not care

for us. We speak of your bringing bad things into our lives, or we wonder why you don't take better care of us. We spend countless hours and resources to make sure our future is secure, but we spend almost no time talking with you about what our future should really look like in order for us to become whole. Forgive us and call us once again by your Spirit into the loving relationship you desire to have with us. Amen.

Leader: God's love is constant and forever. God desires to lead us to wholeness and to life eternal. Receive with joy the loving care of God and continue to draw near to God.

Prayers of the People (and the Lord's Prayer)

We worship and praise your name, O God, for you are the one who has created and redeemed us out of your infinite love for us.

(The following paragraph may be used if a separate prayer of confession has not been used.)

We confess to you, O God, and before one another that we have sinned. You created us out of love and you have become one of us so that we may find salvation in you, and yet we act and talk as if you do not care for us. We speak of your bringing bad things into our lives, or we wonder why you don't take better care of us. We spend countless hours and resources to make sure our future is secure, but we spend almost no time talking with you about what our future should really look like in order for us to become whole. Forgive us and call us once again by your Spirit into the loving relationship you desire to have with us.

We give you thanks for all the ways you have called us to wholeness and life in you. You have been faithful to us in ways beyond our understanding. You have come among us in Jesus and in your Spirit to walk with us and live with us.

You have given us your teaching and have drawn us together into the body of your Christ.

(Other thanksgivings may be offered.)
We pray for those who find it difficult to believe in your loving presence in their lives. There are those who, because of illness or disease, are in distress. Some are grieving loved ones lost to death or to other separations. Some find themselves abused or neglected by those who should be caring for them. Help us, as your people, to reach out to those around us who may need us to make your presence real and alive for them.

(Other intercessions may be offered.)
All these things we ask in the name of our Savior Jesus Christ, who taught us to pray together, saying:
Our Father... Amen.

(Or if the Lord's Prayer is not used at this point in the service)
All this we ask in the name of the Blessed and Holy Trinity. Amen.

Proper 5
Pentecost 3
Ordinary Time 10

1 Kings 17:8-16 (17-24)
Galatians 1:11-24
Luke 7:11-17

Call to Worship
Leader: Let us praise God as long as we live;
People: let us sing praises to God all our life long.
Leader: Happy are those whose help is the God of Jacob,
People: whose hope is in our God.
Leader: God watches over the strangers;
People: God upholds the orphan and the widow.
Leader: God will reign forever.
People: Our God will reign for all generations.

OR

Leader: Come and worship the God of hope!
People: But the world seems so hopeless.
Leader: God comes to bring us life!
People: But we see death and destruction all around us.
Leader: God, who raised Jesus, will raise us to new life as well.
People: Bring us to new life, O God, now and forever.

Hymns and Sacred Songs
"My Hope Is Built"
found in:
UMH: 368   NCH: 403
PH: 379   CH: 537

AAHH: 385   LBW: 293/294
NNBH: 274

"He Touched Me"
found in:
UMH: 367   NNBH: 147
AAHH: 273   CH: 564

"Through It All"
found in:
UMH: 507   CH: 555
NNBH: 402

"It Is Well with My Soul"
found in:
UMH: 377   NCH: 438
AAHH: 377   CH: 561
NNBH: 255

"There Is a Balm in Gilead"
found in:
UMH: 375   NNBH: 489
H82: 676   NCH: 553
PH: 394   CH: 501
AAHH: 524

"Hope of the World"
found in:
UMH: 178   NCH: 46
H82: 472   CH: 538
PH: 360   LBW: 493

"Hymn of Promise"
found in:

UMH: 707   CH: 638
NCH: 433

"O God, Our Help in Ages Past"
found in:
UMH: 117   NCH: 25
H82: 680   CH: 67
AAHH: 170   LBW: 320
NNBH: 46

"All I Need Is You"
found in:
CCB: 100

"People Need the Lord"
found in:
CCB: 52

Prayer for the Day / Collect
O God, who is the hope of all, grant us the faith that enlarges hope, so that we may see the glory you are calling creation to become and so that we can become your glorious instruments of hope; through Jesus Christ our Savior. Amen.

OR

We come to worship and praise our God and to invite God's Spirit to work within us that we might have our faith strengthened and our hope confirmed. Shape us more clearly into your image, O God, and prepare us for your work out in your world for which our Savior Jesus died. Amen.

Prayer of Confession

Leader: Let us confess to God and before one another our sins and especially the way we so easily give up our hope as if we had no one deserving of our faith.

People: **We confess to you, O God, and before one another that we have sinned. We have allowed the stories in the news and the world around us to drain our hope from us. We live as those who have no hope. We despair at the headlines, and we despair for the future of our own lives and families. We celebrate Easter and Pentecost, and then return to our lives and doubt that anything good will come out of this mess we call our world. Forgive our shortsightedness and our inability to focus on our faith in the one who raised Jesus from the dead. Out of death and the fear of the apostles, you brought forth a glorious power through your Spirit. Help us to drink deeply again of that power and be your faithful, hopeful people. Amen.**

Leader: God is already at work in you, raising you to faith and to hope. Receive the power of God's Spirit and live in the joy that is the gift of living in faith.

Prayers of the People (and the Lord's Prayer)

We worship and adore you, O God, because you are the very foundation of our existence. Without the power of your Spirit, all that we have and all that we are would perish.

(The following paragraph may be used if a separate prayer of confession has not been used.)

We confess to you, O God, and before one another that we have sinned. We have allowed the stories in the news and the world around us to drain our hope from us. We live as those who have no hope. We despair at the headlines, and we despair for the future of our own lives and families. We celebrate Easter and Pentecost, and then return to our lives and doubt that anything good will come out of this mess we call our world. Forgive our shortsightedness and our inability to focus on our faith in the one who raised Jesus from the dead. Out of death and the fear of the apostles, you brought forth a glorious power through your Spirit. Help us to drink deeply again of that power and be your faithful, hopeful people.

We give you thanks for all the ways you prove your faithfulness to us. We thank you for the rhythms and seasons of nature. We thank you for the cycle that brings us from conception through maturity to death. We thank you for the countless ways that you show your love and care for us and for all your creation.

(Other thanksgivings may be offered.)
We are very much aware of our needs and the needs of others. There are those who are sick in body and those who are in mourning. There are those who are dying physically and those who are dying spiritually. We know there are people who live with the constant threat of war and death and those who live in hunger and want. As we lift them up to your everlasting care, bless us so that we can be a blessing to those in need around us.

(Other intercessions may be offered.)
All these things we ask in the name of our Savior Jesus Christ, who taught us to pray together, saying:
Our Father... Amen.

(Or if the Lord's Prayer is not used at this point in the service)
All this we ask in the name of the Blessed and Holy Trinity. Amen.

Proper 6
Pentecost 4
Ordinary Time 11

1 Kings 21:1-10 (11-14) 15-21a
Galatians 2:15-21
Luke 7:36—8:3

Call to Worship
Leader: Give ear to our words, O God;
People: give heed to our sighing.
Leader: We enter your house through the abundance of your steadfast love.
People: We bow down in awe of you, our sovereign.
Leader: Lead us in your righteousness;
People: make your way straight before us.

OR

Leader: Come and worship God, the Creator of all.
People: How do we come into the presence of such glory?
Leader: Come with joy, for God loves us.
People: We rejoice in God's presence and celebrate God's love.
Leader: Come with humility, because we are not God!
People: We are aware of our shortcomings and bow before God.

Hymns and Sacred Songs
"I Need Thee Every Hour"
found in:
UMH: 397   NCH: 517

AAHH: 451 CH: 278
NNBH: 303

"Make Me a Captive, Lord"
found in:
UMH: 421 PH: 378

"O Crucified Redeemer"
found in:
UMH: 425

"Behold a Broken World"
found in:
UMH: 426

"Jesu, Jesu"
found in:
UMH: 432 CH: 600
H82: 602 CCB: 66
PH: 367 Renew: 289
NCH: 498

"Cuando El Pore" ("When the Poor Ones")
found in:
UMH: 434 CH: 662
PH: 407

"What Does the Lord Require"
found in:
UMH: 441 PH: 405
H82: 605 CH: 659

"Go Down, Moses"
found in:
UMH: 448 NNBH: 490

PH: 333   CH: 663
AAHH: 543

"Humble Yourself in the Sight of the Lord"
found in:
CCB: 72   Renew: 188

"Make Me a Servant"
found in:
CCB: 90

Prayer for the Day / Collect
O God, who is the sovereign over all creation and yet chose
to come as a servant, grant us the grace and courage to live
our lives honestly instead of lording ourselves over others;
through Jesus Christ, the humble servant. Amen.

OR

We come to worship you, the God who is sovereign of creation as well as its Creator. We come to rejoice in your love
and grace and to bow in adoration of your glory. Help us to
celebrate your love without becoming arrogant and disdain-
ful of our brothers and sisters. Amen.

Prayer of Confession
Leader: Let us confess to God and before one another our
sins and especially the ways we falsely assume that we are
superior to our brothers and sisters.
**People: We confess to you, O God, and before one anoth-
er that we have sinned. You have loved us with a love that
has no bounds, and yet we have loved others with a love
that has many conditions. We judge others and find them
less than ourselves, while you judge them and declare
them your daughters and your sons. Forgive our foolish**

169

haughtiness and bring us once again to the joy of living humbly in the knowledge of who we are in your sight and the esteem of who others are in your sight. Amen.

Leader: God does love us and desires us to live joyfully. God knows we cannot do that if we live in judgment and condemnation. Love God by loving God's children and God's creation.

Prayers of the People (and the Lord's Prayer)

We adore you, O God, and praise you for your greatness. Your power is beyond understanding and your love beyond naming.

(The following paragraph may be used if a separate prayer of confession has not been used.)

We confess to you, O God, and before one another that we have sinned. You have loved us with a love that has no bounds, and yet we have loved others with a love that has many conditions. We judge others and find them less than ourselves, while you judge them and declare them your daughters and your sons. Forgive our foolish haughtiness and bring us once again to the joy of living humbly in the knowledge of who we are in your sight and the esteem of who others are in your sight.

We give you thanks for all the ways you have endowed your creatures and all creation with your majesty. We are truly blessed to be your creatures. You have made us but a little lower than yourself and filled us with your own glory and Spirit.

(Other thanksgivings may be offered.)

We pray for those who have not yet come to understand their own worth in your eyes. We pray for ourselves and others who have belittled others and often done so in your name.

We pray that we may truly be your presence and your blessing to others.

(Other intercessions may be offered.)
All these things we ask in the name of our Savior Jesus Christ, who taught us to pray together, saying:
Our Father... Amen.

(Or if the Lord's Prayer is not used at this point in the service)
All this we ask in the name of the Blessed and Holy Trinity. Amen.

Proper 7
Pentecost 5
Ordinary Time 12

1 Kings 19:1-4 (5-7) 8-15a
Galatians 3:23-29
Luke 8:26-39

Call to Worship
Leader: Come all you who long for God.
People: We thirst for God as a deer thirsts for clear streams.
Leader: Come all who pine for the God of comfort.
People: Our tears have been our food both day and night.
Leader: Why is your soul disquieted within in you?
People: We shall trust in God and praise our helper.

OR

Leader: Come you who are full of fear.
People: It seems that all the powers are against us.
Leader: Come and be fed so that you can be strong.
People: Our strength is almost gone.
Leader: Come and listen for God's voice of utter silence.
People: The silence of God is strength indeed.

Hymns and Sacred Songs
"It Is Well with My Soul"
found in:
UMH: 377   NCH: 438
AAHH: 377   CH: 561
NNBH: 255

"Silence, Frenzied, Unclean Spirit"
found in:
UMH: 264   CH: 186

"Out of the Depths I Cry to You"
found in:
UMH: 515   NCH: 483
H82: 666   CH: 510
PH: 240   LBW: 295

"By Gracious Powers"
found in:
UMH: 517   PH: 342
H82: 695/696   NCH: 413

"O Thou, in Whose Presence"
found in:
UMH: 518

"Lift Every Voice and Sing"
found in:
UMH: 519   NNBH: 457
H82: 599   CH: 631
PH: 563   LBW: 562
AAHH: 540

"Dona Nobis Pacem"
found in:
UMH: 376   CH: 297
H82: 712   Renew: 240

"Great Is Thy Faithfulness"
found in:
UMH: 140   NCH: 423
AAHH: 158   CH: 86

"All I Need Is You"
found in:
CCB: 100

"Fill My Cup, Lord"
found in:
CCB: 47

Prayer for the Day / Collect
O God, who knows us at our best and at our worst, help us to
seek you when things are going well and when life becomes
difficult that we may live our lives in harmony with you;
through Jesus Christ our Savior. Amen.

OR

We come to worship in all the complexities of life. We come
with our joys and with our sorrows. Help us to be open to
your presence, whatever the condition of our lives this day.
Empower us to share your Spirit with others as well. Amen.

Prayer of Confession
Leader: Let us confess to God and before one another our
sins and especially our tendency to forget you when things
go well or to blame you when things get tough.
**People: We confess to you, O God, and before one an-
other that we have sinned. We confess that we allow the
circumstances of our lives to determine our relationship
with you. Whether times are good or bad, we allow those
moments to bend and shape our attitude toward you.
Sometimes things go well and we are grateful, but sometimes when things go well we are pleased with ourselves
and forget you completely. Sometimes when things are**

going badly we find ourselves desperately searching for you, and sometimes we find ourselves blaming you for our situation. Forgive us and help us once more to make our relationship with you the main focus of our lives. Amen.

Leader: God knows that our lives are complicated and that we are creatures of this earth. God loves us and comes to be with us in all the circumstances of our lives. Know that whatever this week brings, God will be there for us all.

Prayers of the People (and the Lord's Prayer)

We come to worship and adore you, our God of salvation. You are the one who transcends all of life and brings to us that holy quality that makes us your children.

(The following paragraph may be used if a separate prayer of confession has not been used.)

We confess to you, O God, and before one another that we have sinned. We confess that we allow the circumstances of our lives to determine our relationship with you. Whether times are good or bad, we allow those moments to bend and shape our attitude toward you. Sometimes things go well and we are grateful, but sometimes when things go well we are pleased with ourselves and forget you completely. Sometimes when things are going badly we find ourselves desperately searching for you, and sometimes we find ourselves blaming you for our situation. Forgive us and help us once more to make our relationship with you the main focus of our lives.

We give you thanks for all the ways you make your presence known to us. We thank you for the beauty of the earth and all creation. We thank you for your loving presence that is shared by our sisters and brothers and strangers. We thank you for the awesome silence that reveals your love to and for us.

(Other thanksgivings may be offered.)
We pray to you for your creation in all its needs. We pray for the earth that we have wounded and for our brothers and sisters we have harmed. We pray for those whose lives seem to fall apart no matter what they do. We pray, most of all, that we may all become more aware of your loving, healing presence in all creation.

(Other intercessions may be offered.)
All these things we ask in the name of our Savior Jesus Christ, who taught us to pray together, saying:
Our Father... Amen.

(Or if the Lord's Prayer is not used at this point in the service)
All this we ask in the name of the Blessed and Holy Trinity. Amen.

Proper 8
Pentecost 6
Ordinary Time 13

2 Kings 2:1-2, 6-14
Galatians 5:1, 13-25
Luke 9:51-62

Call to Worship
Leader: Let us call to mind the deeds of our God.
People: Let us meditate of all God's work and deeds.
Leader: Your way, O God, is holy; who is like you?
People: You are the God who works wonders.
Leader: As your path goes through the sea, we see your footprints.
People: You lead your people with the servants you call forth.

OR

Leader: Come and worship the God who does not change.
People: How can God not change?
Leader: God is steadfast in essence and love.
People: We want to be steadfast in our inner lives.
Leader: God comes to offer us that solid place to stand.
People: With God we will anchor our souls in love.

Hymns and Sacred Songs
"When Our Confidence Is Shaken"
found in:
UMH: 505   CH: 534

"O Thou Who Camest from Above"
found in:
UMH: 501   H82: 704

"Holy, Holy, Holy! Lord God Almighty"
found in:

UMH: 64	NCH: 277
H82: 362	CH: 4
PH: 138	LBW: 165
AAHH: 329	Renew: 204
NNBH: 1	

"Holy God, We Praise Thy Name"
found in:

UMH: 79	NNBH: 13
H82: 366	NCH: 276
PH: 460	LBW: 535

"We Believe in One True God"
found in:
UMH: 85

"We Meet You, O Christ"
found in:

UMH: 257	CH: 183
PH: 311	

"Spirit Song"
found in:

UMH: 347	CCB: 51
AAHH: 321	Renew: 248
CH: 352	

"It Is Well with My Soul"
found in:

UMH: 377 NCH: 438
AAHH: 377 CH: 561
NNBH: 255

"The Steadfast Love of the Lord"
found in:
CCB: 28 Renew: 23

"God, You Are My God"
found in:
CCB: 60

Prayer for the Day / Collect
O God, who is constant yet adaptable to the needs of your
people, grant us the grace to be constant in following our
Savior in the same way while taking on the changes that always confront us; through Jesus Christ our Savior. Amen.

OR

We come to worship you, O God, in the midst of our lives
that are always in turmoil and change. Even as we celebrate
your constant presence, we are aware that you have worked
in myriad ways and through countless people. Help us to be
grounded in you so that we may adapt to the changes around
us. Amen.

Prayer of Confession
Leader: Let us confess to God and before one another our
sins and especially the way we allow the changes of life to
distress us and move us from your way.
**People: We confess to you, O God, and before one an-
other that we have sinned. We have looked at the changes
around us and like the disciples in the boat during the
storm, we cry to you and wonder if you really care for**

us. We call to mind the scripture that you are changeless and expect that our lives will be changeless as well. We forget that it is your nature that does not change and that you have adapted to your creatures time and time again. Center us once again in your constant loving kindness that we may greet our changes from solid footing. So fill us with your Spirit that we may face with courage all that comes our way. Amen.

Leader: God loves us now and God has always loved us. God knows the confusion and turmoil of our lives and invites us once again into the grace of his love. Know that whatever comes our way, our God is with us.

Prayers of the People (and the Lord's Prayer)

We worship and adore you, O God, because you are the changeless one. You are true to your nature of love so that your people proclaim that you are love.

(The following paragraph may be used if a separate prayer of confession has not been used.)

We confess to you, O God, and before one another that we have sinned. We have looked at the changes around us and like the disciples in the boat during the storm, we cry to you and wonder if you really care for us. We call to mind the scripture that you are changeless and expect that our lives will be changeless as well. We forget that it is your nature that does not change and that you have adapted to your creatures time and time again. Center us once again in your constant loving kindness that we may greet our changes from solid footing. So fill us with your Spirit that we may face with courage all that comes our way.

We give you thanks for the constant way you have been with us and for the wonder of changes that have taken place among us. We give you thanks that scientists and thinkers have opened up the mysteries of creation and offered us ways of dealing with sickness that were unknown to those before us. We thank you for the progress that makes our lives easier and more comfortable.

(Other thanksgivings may be offered.)
We pray for those who have been denied the benefits of progress because of tyranny or poverty. We pray for those who are overwhelmed by the changes in their lives. Help us to offer to them the good news of Jesus, which grounds us in your constant loving kindness.

(Other intercessions may be offered.)
All these things we ask in the name of our Savior Jesus Christ, who taught us to pray together, saying:
Our Father... Amen.

(Or if the Lord's Prayer is not used at this point in the service)
All this we ask in the name of the Blessed and Holy Trinity. Amen.

Proper 9
Pentecost 7
Ordinary Time 14

2 Kings 5:1-14
Galatians 6:(1-6) 7-16
Luke 10:1-11, 16-20

Call to Worship
Leader: Sing praise to God, you faithful ones;
People: we give thanks to God's holy name.
Leader: God's anger is but for a moment;
People: God's favor is for a lifetime.
Leader: God has turned our mourning into dancing;
People: so we will give thanks to God forever.

OR

Leader: Come and worship the Creator of all.
People: We are not worthy to come before God.
Leader: God created you and called you good.
People: You are right. We are pretty special.
Leader: We are special to God, but we are also sinful.
People: We come before God in humility, confessing who we are.

Hymns and Sacred Songs
"It's Me, It's Me, O Lord"
found in:
UMH: 352   CH: 579
NNBH: 496

"Pues Si Vivimos" ("When We Are Living")
found in:

UMH: 356	NCH: 499
PH: 400	CH: 536

"All People that on Earth Do Dwell"
found in:

UMH: 75	NNBH: 7
H82: 377/378	NCH: 18
AAHH: 36	CH: 245

"How Great Thou Art"
found in:

UMH: 77	CH: 33
PH: 467	LBW: 532
AAHH: 148	Renew: 250
NNBH: 43	

"Maker, in Whom We Live"
found in:
UMH: 88

"Immortal, Invisible, God Only Wise"
found in:

UMH: 103	CH: 66
H82: 423	LBW: 526
PH: 263	Renew: 46
NCH: 1	

"God of the Sparrow, God of the Whale"
found in:

UMH: 122	NCH: 32
PH: 272	CH: 70

"Make Me a Captive, Lord"
found in:
UMH: 421   PH: 378

"Great Is the Lord"
found in:
CCB: 65   Renew: 22

"Make Me a Servant"
found in:
CCB: 90

Prayer for the Day / Collect

O God, who created us and knows that our frame is but dust, grant us the wisdom to remember who we are and to live in the knowledge that we are creatures of the earth who are filled with divine life; through Jesus Christ our Savior. Amen.

OR

We come to offer our praise and worship to you, the God who created us. You made us out of the dust of the earth and yet formed us into your own image. Give us the wisdom of your Spirit that in true humility we may live in the truth of both our gifts and our flaws. Amen.

Prayer of Confession

Leader: Let us confess to God and before one another our sins and especially our inability to live in humility before you and with one another.
People: We confess to you, O God, and before one another that we have sinned. Finding ourselves in your image, we begin to think that we are gods. We want to make the rules and call the shots in our lives and the lives of those around us. We forget that we are your creatures and not

our own creators. At other times we are painfully aware of our mortality and sinfulness and think of ourselves as nothing. We despair at the lack of power we have over our own lives. In both of these we have lost humility, the ability to live in the truth of who we are. Grant that by the power of your Spirit we may joyfully accept our place as your creatures who are also your children. Help us to treat others with the same dignity that you offer us. Amen.

Leader: God knows who we are — we are both gifted and flawed. God knows our weakness and our strength. God loves us as we are and invites us to do the same.

Prayers of the People (and the Lord's Prayer)

We praise and glorify your name, O God, for you are the one who created us out of the dust of the earth and filled us with your own Spirit, breath, and life. You know us better than we know ourselves.

(The following paragraph may be used if a separate prayer of confession has not been used.)

We confess to you, O God, and before one another that we have sinned. Finding ourselves in your image, we begin to think that we are gods. We want to make the rules and call the shots in our lives and the lives of those around us. We forget that we are your creatures and not our own creators. At other times we are painfully aware of our mortality and sinfulness and think of ourselves as nothing. We despair at the lack of power we have over our own lives. In both of these we have lost humility, the ability to live in the truth of who we are. Grant that by the power of your Spirit we may joyfully accept our place as your creatures who are also your children. Help us to treat others with the same dignity that you offer us.

We give you thanks for all the ways you have blessed us. As creatures, you have given us the ability to sense the world around us. You have made us able to enjoy the smell of roses, spring rain, and burnt toast. You made us able to feel the rough texture of wool, the softness of silk, and the warmth of another's body. You gave us the sense of taste so that we can experience sweet, sour, and salty. You have opened us to sounds of laughter, crying, and music. We are created to see the sunrise and sunset, the starry heavens, and a newborn baby. You have made us so like yourself that we can experience your presence beyond these senses.

(Other thanksgivings may be offered.)
Aware of all the care with which you made us, we are confident in your care not only for us but for all creation. We offer up to you those who have lost their sense of wonder at all that is about them because they have experienced so much pain and violence in their lives. We offer to your care those who have not discovered your presence with and within them. We offer ourselves to you that we may be part of their healing.

(Other intercessions may be offered.)
All these things we ask in the name of our Savior Jesus Christ, who taught us to pray together, saying:
Our Father... Amen.

(Or if the Lord's Prayer is not used at this point in the service)
All this we ask in the name of the Blessed and Holy Trinity. Amen.

Proper 10
Pentecost 8
Ordinary Time 15

Amos 7:7-17
Colossians 1:1-14
Luke 10:25-37

Call to Worship
Leader: God demands that we give up injustice and partiality.
People: We must give justice to the weak and the orphan.
Leader: We must maintain the right of the lowly and destitute.
People: We must rescue the weak and the needy.
Leader: Rise up, O God, and judge the earth.
People: All the nations belong to our God!

OR

Leader: God calls us to worship in spirit and in truth.
People: We are ready to hear the truth of God.
Leader: God calls us to hear the truth about ourselves.
People: We are not so ready to hear that truth.
Leader: When we accept the truth about ourselves, we are freed.
People: We shall listen to the truth and it shall set us free.

Hymns and Sacred Songs
"Holy, Holy, Holy!"
found in:

UMH: 64   NCH: 277
H82: 362   CH: 4
PH: 138   LBW: 165
AAHH: 329   Renew: 204
NNBH: 1

"Holy God, We Praise Thy Name"
found in:
UMH: 79   NNBH: 13
H82: 366   NCH: 276
PH: 460   LBW: 535

"Immortal, Invisible, God Only Wise"
found in:
UMH: 103   CH: 66
H82: 423   LBW: 526
PH: 263   Renew: 46
NCH: 1

"Breathe on Me, Breath of God"
found in:
UMH: 420   NNBH: 126
H82: 508   NCH: 292
PH: 316   CH: 254
AAHH: 317   LBW: 488

"I Want a Principle Within"
found in:
UMH: 410

"Lord, I Want to Be a Christian"
found in:
UMH: 402   NCH: 456
PH: 372   CH: 589

AAHH: 463   Renew: 145
NNBH: 156

"Take My Life, and Let It Be"
found in:
UMH: 399   NCH: 448
H82: 707   CH: 609
PH: 391   LBW: 406
NNBH: 213   Renew: 150

"Take Time to Be Holy"
found in:
UMH: 395   CH: 572
NNBH: 306

"Sing Unto the Lord a New Song"
found in:
CCB: 16

"Refiner's Fire"
found in:
CCB: 79

Prayer for the Day / Collect
O God, who is truth, grant us the courage to hear the truth
about ourselves and to act on that truth; through Jesus Christ
our Savior. Amen.

OR

We come into the presence of pure truth and we know that
we are people who play fast and loose with truth. Help us as
we worship you, O God, to let go of our deceitfulness and to
be open to your cleansing Holy Spirit. Amen.

Prayer of Confession

Leader: Let us confess to God and before one another our sins and especially the way we so easily bend the truth to our advantage.

People: We confess to you, O God, and before one another that we have sinned. We are a people who talk about valuing truth, and yet we are quick to bend the truth for our own purposes. We rationalize our lying and tell ourselves that we are really honest people who just need to shade the truth for a really good reason. Open our eyes that we may see the truth about ourselves and so fill us with your Spirit that we are able to truly repent and become people of truth. Amen.

Leader: God is Spirit and truth and desires us to be the same. Step into the truth of God and live from there.

Prayers of the People (and the Lord's Prayer)

We worship and adore you, O God, for you are the one who is whole and complete. There is no deception in you and your actions mirror your nature.

(The following paragraph may be used if a separate prayer of confession has not been used.)

We confess to you, O God, and before one another that we have sinned. We are a people who talk about valuing truth, and yet we are quick to bend the truth for our own purposes. We rationalize our lying and tell ourselves that we are really honest people who just need to shade the truth for a really good reason. Open our eyes that we may see the truth about ourselves and so fill us with your Spirit that we are able to truly repent and become people of truth.

We give you thanks for showing us the way of truth in Jesus Christ. You invite us to live in the truth of who we are and of who we are to become. We thank you for the good creation and the ways it reveals its truths to us.

(Other thanksgivings may be offered.)
We pray for ourselves and all who live in self-deception. Free us from the need to lie about ourselves to others and to ourselves. So fill us with the knowledge of your love and grace that we accept ourselves and one another and grow in your likeness.

(Other intercessions may be offered.)
All these things we ask in the name of our Savior Jesus Christ, who taught us to pray together, saying:
Our Father... Amen.

(Or if the Lord's Prayer is not used at this point in the service)
All this we ask in the name of the Blessed and Holy Trinity. Amen.

Proper 11
Pentecost 9
Ordinary Time 16

Amos 8:1-12
Colossians 1:15-28
Luke 10:38-42

Call to Worship
Leader: We trust in the steadfast love of God forever,
People: and so we are like the green olive trees.
Leader: Let us gives thanks to God forever.
People: We give thanks for all that God has done.
Leader: Let us come into the presence of the faithful.
People: Let us proclaim the good name of God.

OR

Leader: Come before the God who gives us freedom.
People: We worship the one who gives us choices.
Leader: With the freedom of choice comes responsibility.
People: We must live with the consequences of our choices.
Leader: God desires us to choose life over death.
People: We shall listen to God's word that we may choose wisely.

Hymns and Sacred Songs
"God Hath Spoken by the Prophets"
found in:
UMH: 108

"Spirit Song"
found in:

UMH: 347	CH: 352
AAHH: 321	Renew: 248

"Dear Lord and Father of Mankind"
found in:

UMH: 358	NCH: 502
H82: 652/653	CH: 594
PH: 345	LBW: 506

"Savior, Like a Shepherd Lead Us"
found in:

UMH: 381	NNBH: 54
H82: 708	NCH: 252
PH: 387	CH: 558
AAHH: 424	LBW: 481

"This Is a Day of New Beginnings"
found in:

UMH: 383	CH: 518
NCH: 417	

"O Come and Dwell in Me"
found in:
UMH: 388

"O Happy Day, that Fixed My Choice"
found in:

UMH: 391	NNBH: 373
AAHH: 359	

"Take Time to Be Holy"
found in:

UMH: 395   CH: 572
NNBH: 306

"Shine, Jesus, Shine"
found in:
CCB: 81   Renew: 247

"Open Our Eyes, Lord"
found in:
CCB: 77   Renew: 91

Prayer for the Day / Collect
O God, who gives to your creatures the ability to choose, grant us the wisdom to make good choices so that our choices help us love you more and help us take care of our neighbors near and far; through Jesus Christ our Savior. Amen.

OR

O God, you have made us with the freedom to choose. Your love for us is so great that you would risk our rejecting you rather than force us to love you. We thank you for our freedom and pray that you would also grant us wisdom and courage to choose rightly. Amen.

Prayer of Confession
Leader: Let us confess to God and before one another our sins and especially the ways we misuse our freedom to choose.
People: We confess to you, O God, and before one another that we have sinned. You have given us the freedom to choose so that we might fully enter into a loving relationship with you and with one another. Yet we use our freedom to choose things over relationships. We worship objects and use people. We use our freedom to ignore you and to follow the way to death and destruction. Forgive

us our foolish ways and empower us with your Spirit that
we might choose life in, with, and for you. Amen.
Leader: God honors our freedom to choose and is always
pleased when we choose him, love, and neighbors. Live in
the power to choose wisely and well.

Prayers of the People (and the Lord's Prayer)
We worship you, O creating God, who lovingly gives your
creatures the ability to choose. We praise you for your love
and never-failing care.

*(The following paragraph may be used if a separate prayer
of confession has not been used.)*
We confess to you, O God, and before one another that we
have sinned. You have given us the freedom to choose so that
we might fully enter into a loving relationship with you and
with one another. Yet we use our freedom to choose things
over relationships. We worship objects and use people. We
use our freedom to ignore you and to follow the way to death
and destruction. Forgive us our foolish ways and empower
us with your Spirit that we might choose life in, with, and
for you.

We thank you for your love that desires our good and our
growth. We thank you for the church and the way in which
we have been nurtured in the faith. We thank you most of
all for your presence incarnate in this world, which gives us
direction, hope, and life.

(Other thanksgivings may be offered.)
We pray for all who have difficult decisions to make. There
are many options out there and it is so easy to choose foolishly. Help all of us to make the choices that lead to abundant
life in you.

(Other intercessions may be offered.)
All these things we ask in the name of our Savior Jesus Christ, who taught us to pray together, saying:
Our Father... Amen.

(Or if the Lord's Prayer is not used at this point in the service)
All this we ask in the name of the Blessed and Holy Trinity. Amen.

Proper 12
Pentecost 10
Ordinary Time 17

Hosea 1:2-10
Colossians 2:6-15 (16-19)
Luke 11:1-13

Call to Worship
Leader: God has forgiven all our iniquities;
People: God has pardoned all our sins.
Leader: Restore us again, O God of salvation;
People: put away your indignation toward us.
Leader: Steadfast love and faithfulness will meet.
People: Righteousness and peace will kiss each other.

OR

Leader: God calls us to enter into life that is full of glory.
People: How do we enter this life?
Leader: God has sent us Jesus to show us the way.
People: Tell us about Jesus so that we may follow him.
Leader: You must know him in your heart, as well as your head.
People: We invite the Christ into our hearts to lead us to life.

Hymns and Sacred Songs
"O Come and Dwell in Me"
found in:
UMH: 388

"Spirit of the Living God"
found in:
UMH: 393   NCH: 283
PH: 322   CCB: 57
AAHH: 320   Renew: 90
NNBH: 133

"Something Beautiful"
found in:
UMH: 394   CH: 299
PH: 565/573 Renew: 145

"I Am Thine, O Lord"
found in:
UMH: 419   NCH: 455
AAHH: 387   CH: 601
NNBH: 202

"Let There Be Peace on Earth"
found in:
UMH: 431   CH: 677

"Be Thou My Vision"
found in:
UMH: 451   NCH: 451
H82: 488   CH: 595
PH: 339   Renew: 151

"More Love to Thee, O Christ"
found in:
UMH: 453   NNBH: 214
PH: 359   NCH: 456
AAHH: 575   CH: 527

"All Hail King Jesus"
found in:
CCB: 29
Renew: 35

"Turn Your Eyes Upon Jesus"
found in:
CCB: 55

Prayer for the Day / Collect
O God, who created us and desires nothing more than for us
to have eternal life, grant us the wisdom and courage to follow Jesus so that we may know you and your life more fully
through Jesus Christ our Savior. Amen.

OR

We come into your presence, O God of creation, so that we
might praise you and enter into your life now and forever.
Open our hearts and minds to the message of Jesus, so that
we might follow him with love and devotion this day and all
our days. Amen.

Prayer of Confession
Leader: Let us confess to God and before one another our
sins and especially the ways we are content to allow our faith
to be only in our heads and not in our hearts.
**People: We confess to you, O God, and before one another
that we have sinned. We have claimed to be your people
with our mouths, but our hearts betray us to the truth
that we have centered our lives on things other than you.
We have filled our time and our hearts with greed, retaliation, and anger and have not allowed Jesus to purge us
of our sins. Forgive us and empower us with your Spirit**

to open our hearts to the cleansing fire of our Savior that we may truly be your children. Amen.

Leader: From the moment the divine breath, Spirit, wind entered into humankind, God has desired to dwell fully within us. God hears your prayer and grants you his Spirit so that you may allow the Christ to dwell in you fully.

Prayers of the People (and the Lord's Prayer)

We worship and adore you, O God, for you have created us to be the residence of your own presence and Spirit. You have made us to be filled with yourself and placed us here to be your image, your ambassadors.

(The following paragraph may be used if a separate prayer of confession has not been used.)

We confess to you, O God, and before one another that we have sinned. We have claimed to be your people with our mouths, but our hearts betray us to the truth that we have centered our lives on things other than you. We have filled our time and our hearts with greed, retaliation, and anger and have not allowed Jesus to purge us of our sins. Forgive us and empower us with your Spirit to open our hearts to the cleansing fire of our Savior that we may truly be your children.

We give you thanks for all the ways we find your presence and power in and among us. We thank you for those who have been faithful in allowing Christ to live in them so that we found ourselves drawn to you.

(Other thanksgivings may be offered.)

We pray for all your creatures that we may learn to turn to the power of the Christ who comes to dwell in us and transform us into the glory you created us to be. Help us who call ourselves Christians to truly be those who indwell with the presence of the Christ.

200

(Other intercessions may be offered.)
All these things we ask in the name of our Savior Jesus
Christ, who taught us to pray together, saying:
Our Father... Amen.

(Or if the Lord's Prayer is not used at this point in the ser-
vice)
All this we ask in the name of the Blessed and Holy Trinity.
Amen.

Proper 13
Pentecost 11
Ordinary Time 18

Hosea 11:1-11
Colossians 3:1-11
Luke 12:13-21

Call to Worship
Leader: Give thanks to God who is good;
People: God's steadfast love endures forever.
Leader: God satisfies the thirsty;
People: and the hungry God fills with good things.
Leader: Let those who are wise give heed to this.
People: Let us consider the steadfast love of our God.

OR

Leader: Come to the God who calls us home.
People: Sometimes the call of God is scary.
Leader: Do not be afraid. Remember the words of Jesus.
People: We recall the love God spoke about.
Leader: Hear now as God calls you home.
People: With joy we return to the God who loves us.

Hymns and Sacred Songs
"Joyful, Joyful, We Adore Thee"
found in:

UMH: 89	NNBH: 40
H82: 376	NCH: 4
PH: 464	CH: 2
AAHH: 120	LBW: 551

"God, Whose Love Is Reigning O'er Us"
found in:
UMH: 100

"The Care the Eagle Gives Her Young"
found in:
UMH: 118   CH: 76
NCH: 468

"Your Love, O God"
found in:
UMH: 120

"Softly and Tenderly Jesus Is Calling"
found in:
UMH: 348   NCH: 449
AAHH: 347   CH: 340
NNBH: 168   Renew: 147

"Love Divine, All Loves Excelling"
found in:
UMH: 384   NCH: 43
H82: 657   CH: 517
PH: 376   LBW: 316
AAHH: 440   Renew: 196
NNBH: 65

"Jesus Calls Us"
found in:
UMH: 398   NCH: 171/172
H82: 549/550   CH: 337
NNBH: 183   LBW: 494

"Thou Hidden Love of God"
found in:
UMH: 414

"Awesome God"
found in:
CCB: 17   Renew: 245

"More Precious than Silver"
found in:
CCB: 25

Prayer for the Day / Collect
O God, who desires more than anything to give us abundant life, help us to hear your roar as an invitation to life and not as an attack on us; through Jesus Christ our Savior. Amen.

OR

O God, who desires more than anything to give us abundant life, help us to discern the truly good things you offer us so that we may find ourselves rich toward you whether we have much or little of this world's goods; through Jesus Christ our Savior. Amen.

OR

We come to worship you, O God, the one who loves us more than life itself. We come to learn more about you so that we can love you more fully, and we come to learn of the way of Jesus so that we might come to full and abundant life in you. Amen.

Prayer of Confession

Leader: Let us confess to God and before one another our sins and especially the way we are so quick to assign our motives to God.

People: We confess to you, O God, and before one another that we have sinned. We focus our lives on the accumulation of goods and say it is part of your plan for our lives; yet we ignore the needs of the poor. We detest others and condemn them in your name. We allow our wants and desires to rule our lives and then claim that this is your will. Forgive us for our blatant misuse of you and of our brothers and sisters. Restore us in the power of your Spirit that we may learn once again to listen to our Savior and follow the way of the Christ. Amen.

Leader: God is always calling his wayward children home. God desires only that we come to eternal life and bring our sisters and brothers with us.

Prayers of the People (and the Lord's Prayer)

We worship and praise your name, O God, because you are the Creator and redeemer of all creation. You are the one who calls us home.

(The following paragraph may be used if a separate prayer of confession has not been used.)

We confess to you, O God, and before one another that we have sinned. We focus our lives on the accumulation of goods and say it is part of your plan for our lives; yet we ignore the needs of the poor. We detest others and condemn them in your name. We allow our wants and desires to rule our lives and then claim that this is your will. Forgive us for our blatant misuse of you and of our brothers and sisters. Restore us in the power of your Spirit that we may learn once again to listen to our Savior and follow the way of the Christ.

We thank you for all the ways you share your love with us. We thank you for the good creation and all the blessings it offers us. We thank you for one another and the blessings we receive when we take care of our neighbors, near and far. We thank you for your loving kindness that always seeks us and the good of all your creatures.

(Other thanksgivings may be offered.)
We pray to you for one another in our need and for all, anywhere, who have wandered far from their home in you. As you are about the work of calling your children home, use us to be part of that loving call. Enable us to echo your call in ways that cause others to understand your great love for all of us.

(Other intercessions may be offered.)
All these things we ask in the name of our Savior Jesus Christ, who taught us to pray together, saying:
Our Father... Amen.

(Or if the Lord's Prayer is not used at this point in the service)
All this we ask in the name of the Blessed and Holy Trinity. Amen.

Proper 14
Pentecost 12
Ordinary Time 19

Isaiah 1:1, 10-20
Hebrews 11:1-3, 8-16
Luke 12:32-40

Call to Worship
Leader: The mighty one, our God, speaks and summons the earth.
People: Out of Zion, God shines forth as perfection.
Leader: The heavens declare God's righteousness.
People: God alone is our judge.
Leader: Those who bring thanksgiving honor God.
People: To these, God will show salvation.

OR

Leader: Come and worship the God who created us.
People: We come as but dust of the earth.
Leader: Come and worship the God who is within us.
People: We come as the holy children of God.
Leader: Come and worship the God who became one of us.
People: We come acknowledging that we are dust and spirit.

Hymns and Sacred Songs
"All Creatures of Our God and King"
found in:
UMH: 62   NCH: 17
H82: 400   CH: 22
PH: 455   LBW: 527

AAHH: 147   Renew: 47
NNBH: 33

"From All that Dwell Below the Skies"
found in:

UMH: 101	NCH: 27
H82: 380	CH: 49
PH: 229	LBW: 550

"Many Gifts, One Spirit"
found in:

UMH: 114	NCH: 177

"It's Me, It's Me, O Lord"
found in:

UMH: 352	CH: 579
NNBH: 496	

"Like the Murmur of the Dove's Song"
found in:

UMH: 544	NCH: 270
H82: 513	CH: 245
PH: 314	Renew: 280

"Where Charity and Love Prevail"
found in:

UMH: 549	NCH: 396
H82: 581	LBW: 126

"Take My Life, and Let It Be"
found in:

UMH: 399	NCH: 448
H82: 707	CH: 609
PH: 391	LBW: 406
NNBH: 213	Renew: 150

"Just As I Am, Without One Plea"
found in:
UMH: 357   NCH: 207
H82: 693   CH: 339
PH: 370   LBW: 296
AAHH: 344/345   Renew: 140
NNBH: 167

"Refiner's Fire"
found in:
CCB: 79

"God, You Are My God"
found in:
CCB: 60

In the end, all we can ever sing is "Kyrie Eleison."

Prayer for the Day / Collect
O God, who created us out of common dirt and divine breath, grant us the wisdom to accept ourselves as being gifted and flawed and to move ever closer to your image through Jesus Christ our Savior. Amen.

OR

We have come to worship you, O God, our Creator and our redeemer. We come with all our flaws and with all the potential you created within us. Help us to listen to you this day so that we might live more fully into your image this week. Amen.

Prayer of Confession
Leader: Let us confess to God and before one another our sins and especially our fascination with the extremes of life.

People: We confess to you, O God, and before one another that we have sinned. We find ourselves drawn ever to the weird and the wonderful in the news. We are fascinated with the extreme cruelties our sisters and brothers commit as well as the wondrous good things they do. We are also locked into the extremes in our own lives. Sometimes we think we are much better than we really are and we look down our noses at others. Sometimes we think we are much worse than we are and we beat ourselves up. Forgive our foolishness and help us see ourselves as you see us: sinners with divine potential. Help us then to live so that others discover the same wonder about themselves. Amen.

Leader: God knows us and loves us in all our wonderful and awful moments. As God loves us and accepts us, so may the Spirit empower you to love and accept yourselves and each other.

Prayers of the People (and the Lord's Prayer)

We worship and praise you, O God, Creator and redeemer of all creation. We praise you for your loving kindness, which has created us with great potential and accepts us in our sinfulness.

(The following paragraph may be used if a separate prayer of confession has not been used.)

We confess to you, O God, and before one another that we have sinned. We find ourselves drawn ever to the weird and the wonderful in the news. We are fascinated with the extreme cruelties our sisters and brothers commit as well as the wondrous good things they do. We are also locked into the extremes in our own lives. Sometimes we think we are much better than we really are and we look down our noses at others. Sometimes we think we are much worse than we are and we beat ourselves up. Forgive our foolishness and help us see ourselves as you see us: sinners with divine potential. Help us then to live so that others discover the same wonder about themselves.

We give you thanks for all the ways you have called us and our sisters and brothers to realize the potential of your image embedded deeply within us. We thank you for those who have reached beyond their selfish sinfulness and offered love and hope to us and to others. Most of all we thank you for Jesus, who shows us how to live fully as your children.

(Other thanksgivings may be offered.)
We pray for each other in our need. We especially pray for the wisdom and the courage to live more into your image each day. We pray for ourselves and for others that we may all see your loving goal for our lives.

(Other intercessions may be offered.)
All these things we ask in the name of our Savior Jesus Christ, who taught us to pray together, saying:
Our Father... Amen.

(Or if the Lord's Prayer is not used at this point in the service)
All this we ask in the name of the Blessed and Holy Trinity. Amen.

Proper 15
Pentecost 13
Ordinary Time 20

Isaiah 5:1-7
Hebrews 11:29—12:2
Luke 12:49-56

Call to Worship
Leader: Give ear, O Shepherd of Israel.
People: Stir up your might and come and save us.
Leader: Let your hand, O God, be upon us.
People: Then we will never turn away from you.
Leader: Restore us and let your face shine upon us.
People: Let your face shine upon us that we may be saved.

OR

Leader: Take courage, the witnesses are all around us.
People: We give thanks for those who have been faithful.
Leader: They have lived their faith in all conditions.
People: They are like beacons calling us to faithfulness.
Leader: Will others find us to be the light they need in dark times?
People: In humility, we will strive to live so that they will.

OR

Leader: Jesus calls us to come to him.
People: We answer the call and come for healing.

Leader: Healing you will receive — and much more.
People: What else does Jesus have for us?
Leader: He calls us to stand with him against hatred and evil.
People: We will stand against these with the Christ.
Leader: Sometimes that will mean standing against family and friends.
People: God, grant us the courage to stand with Jesus always.

Hymns and Sacred Songs
"Ye Servants of God"
found in:

UMH: 181	NCH: 305
H82: 535	CH: 110
PH: 477	LBW: 252

"Hope of the World"
found in:

UMH: 178	NCH: 46
H82: 472	CH: 538
PH: 360	LBW: 493

"Stand Up, Stand Up for Jesus"
found in:

UMH: 514	NNBH: 409
H82: 561	CH: 613
AAHH: 476	LBW: 389

"Am I a Soldier of the Cross"
found in:

UMH: 511	NNBH: 259
AAHH: 482/483, 603	

"Are Ye Able"
found in:
UMH: 530   CH: 621
NNBH: 223

"Filled with the Spirit's Power"
found in:
UMH: 537   LBW: 160
NCH: 266

"Must Jesus Bear the Cross Alone"
found in:
UMH: 424   NNBH: 221
AAHH: 554

"Take Up Thy Cross"
found in:
UMH: 415   PH: 393
H82: 675   LBW: 398

"Shine, Jesus, Shine"
found in:
CCB: 81   Renew: 247

"God, You Are My God"
found in:
CCB: 60

Prayer for the Day / Collect
O God, who sent Jesus to announce and bring your reign, grant us the courage to stand with him even when it is unpopular; through Jesus Christ our Savior. Amen.

OR

O God, who has given us the witness of countless faithful ones, grant us the courage to so live that we too can be faithful witnesses for you; through Jesus Christ our Savior. Amen.

OR

As we come into your presence, O God, to offer our worship and praise, we are aware of the presence of your faithful ones all around us. Help us to clearly hear your word to us this day so that we may choose true witnesses to help us model our lives for you. Amen.

Prayer of Confession
Leader: Let us confess to God and before one another our sins and especially the way we honor people whose stance is not that of our Savior.

People: We confess to you, O God, and before one another that we have sinned. We look with admiration on those who have amassed great wealth or power or popularity, without regarding how they have gained these things. We honor sports figures who live lifestyles that abuse their bodies and other people. When we hear of those who have given themselves in the causes of the reign of God, we may be amazed for a short time but we feel no desire to be like them. Forgive us our double-mindedness and call us once more to stand with Jesus as bearers of your gracious reign. Amen.

Leader: Jesus opens the reign of God to all, even those of us who have wavered in our faithfulness. Welcome into God's world. Live always as God's ambassadors.

Prayers of the People (and the Lord's Prayer)

We praise and worship you, the God who brings all creation to its completeness. Your gracious desire is always for the abundant life of your creation and your creatures.

(The following paragraph may be used if a separate prayer of confession has not been used.)

We confess to you, O God, and before one another that we have sinned. We look with admiration on those who have amassed great wealth or power or popularity, without regarding how they have gained these things. We honor sports figures who live lifestyles that abuse their bodies and other people. When we hear of those who have given themselves in the causes of the reign of God, we may be amazed for a short time but we feel no desire to be like them. Forgive us our double-mindedness and call us once more to stand with Jesus as bearers of your gracious reign.

We thank you for all the signs you send us to help us live into the fullness of your reign. We thank you especially for those saints who will never be remembered in history books but who made such a difference in our lives.

(Other thanksgivings may be offered.)

We pray for those who face great opposition to their faithfully living in your reign. We pray for those who are imprisoned or martyred for your sake. We pray for those who are mocked and ridiculed for upholding your standards. We pray for ourselves and the courage to follow their example.

(Other intercessions may be offered.)

All these things we ask in the name of our Savior Jesus Christ, who taught us to pray together, saying:
Our Father... Amen.

(Or if the Lord's Prayer is not used at this point in the service)
All this we ask in the name of the Blessed and Holy Trinity. Amen.

Proper 16
Pentecost 14
Ordinary Time 21

Jeremiah 1:4-10
Hebrews 12:18-29
Luke 13:10-17

Call to Worship
Leader: Let us take refuge in our God.
People: In God we will never be put to shame.
Leader: Let God be our rock and our refuge.
People: God is our hope, our trust.
Leader: Let us lean upon our God.
People: Our praise is continually of our God.

OR

Leader: Come and serve the one who calls you.
People: We come and offer ourselves to God.
Leader: God calls us to give our all to his reign.
People: We are willing to sacrifice all for God.
Leader: Only for the good news of God are you called.
People: Only for God's good news do we offer our lives.

Hymns and Sacred Songs
"O for a Heart to Praise My God"
found in:
UMH: 417

"I Want a Principle Within"
found in:
UMH: 410

"The Gift of Love"
found in:
UMH: 408   CH: 526
AAHH: 522   Renew: 155

"Jesu, Jesu"
found in:
UMH: 432   CH: 600
H82: 602   CCB: 66
PH: 367   Renew: 289
NCH: 498

"Let There Be Peace on Earth"
found in:
UMH: 431   CH: 677

"All People that on Earth Do Dwell"
found in:
UMH: 75   NCH: 7
H82: 377/379   CH: 18
PH: 220/221   LBW: 245
NNBH: 36

"We, Thy People, Praise Thee"
found in:
UMH: 67

"Word of God, Come Down on Earth"
found in:
UMH: 182

"Turn Your Eyes Upon Jesus"
found in:
CCB: 55

"Our God Reigns"
found in:
CCB: 33

Prayer for the Day / Collect
O God, who calls us from before our creation, grant us the wisdom to know the difference between the times when our calling as your disciples requires sacrifice and when it is only the ego of ourselves or others that demands it; through Jesus Christ our Savior. Amen.

OR

We have come to worship you, O God, and to receive our marching orders as disciples of Jesus. Help us in the time of worship to discern rightly what it is that you require of us, so that we may be faithful to you and not be destroyed by our own misunderstandings. Amen.

OR

O God, who calls us to become completely transparent to your presence, grant us the wisdom and courage to seek that transparency even when it means giving up our understanding of how things are supposed to be; through Jesus Christ our Savior. Amen.

Prayer of Confession
Leader: Let us confess to God and before one another our sins and especially the way we cling to our principles even when they destroy others.
People: We confess to you, O God, and before one another that we have sinned. We have taken the words of life you have given us and used them as weapons against our sisters and brothers. We have taken a stance of holiness

to block the way of the Holy One. You have called us to become living sacrifices for your reign, but we often sacrifice ourselves for our own status. Forgive us our self-centered ways and call us once more to be transformed into your image, so that we may wisely use your truths to bring us and the whole world closer to you. Amen.

Leader: God desires the salvation of all creation and welcomes us even when we have been unfaithful. God grants us forgiveness and invites us once more to join in the work of salvation.

Prayers of the People (and the Lord's Prayer)

We worship and sing your praises, O God, because you are the one who calls us. You call us to serve you and to serve our sisters and brothers.

(The following paragraph may be used if a separate prayer of confession has not been used.)

We confess to you, O God, and before one another that we have sinned. We have taken the words of life you have given us and used them as weapons against our sisters and brothers. We have taken a stance of holiness to block the way of the Holy One. You have called us to become living sacrifices for your reign, but we often sacrifice ourselves for our own status. Forgive us our self-centered ways and call us once more to be transformed into your image, so that we may wisely use your truths to bring us and the whole world closer to you.

We give you thanks for all those who have been true to the task of being transformed into your image. There have been those holy ones in our lives who were willing to risk ridicule and rejection because they loved you more than the signs that point to you. They sacrificed themselves as they became more radiant with your glory. They resisted the siren call to please others.

(Other thanksgivings may be offered.)
We pray for one another in our need. We pray especially for those who find themselves being used up not for your reign but for the pleasure of those who demand so much of them. We pray for those who have gotten so entangled in the signs you have sent that they no longer can see you. We pray especially for ourselves that we may be faithful to you and to those you have given us to serve.

(Other intercessions may be offered.)
All these things we ask in the name of our Savior Jesus Christ, who taught us to pray together, saying:
Our Father . . . Amen.

(Or if the Lord's Prayer is not used at this point in the service)
All this we ask in the name of the Blessed and Holy Trinity. Amen.

Proper 17
Pentecost 15
Ordinary Time 22

Jeremiah 2:4-13
Hebrews 13:1-8, 15-16
Luke 14:1, 7-14

Call to Worship
Leader: Sing aloud to God our strength;
People: shout for joy to the God of Jacob.
Leader: God is the one who brought us out of bondage.
People: But we did not listen to God.
Leader: God desires that we listen and live.
People: Only then will we be truly satisfied.

OR

Leader: Come and join with Jesus.
People: We follow our exalted head.
Leader: Come and join with Jesus the servant.
People: We go with Jesus to serve others.
Leader: Come and join with Jesus the despised.
People: We take on shame and abuse for God's reign.

Hymns and Sacred Songs
"O Master, Let Me Walk with Thee"
found in:
UMH: 430
H82: 659/660
PH: 357
NNBH: 445

NCH: 503
CH: 602
LBW: 492

223

"Cuando El Pobre" ("When the Poor Ones")
found in:
UMH: 434   CH: 662
PH: 407

"What Does the Lord Require"
found in:
UMH: 441   PH: 405
H82: 605   CH: 659

"Lift High the Cross"
found in:
UMH: 159   NCH: 198
H82: 473   CH: 108
PH: 371   LBW: 377
AAHH: 242   Renew: 297

"O Love, How Deep"
found in:
UMH: 267   NCH: 209
H82: 448/449   LBW: 88
PH: 83

"O Zion, Haste"
found in:
UMH: 573   NNBH: 422
H82: 539   LBW: 397

"God of Love and God of Power"
found in:
UMH: 578

"When the Church of Jesus"
found in:
UMH: 592   CH: 470

"The Steadfast Love of the Lord"
found in:
CCB: 28   Renew: 23

"We Are His Hands"
found in:
CCB: 85

"Make Me a Servant"
found in:
CCB: 90

Prayer for the Day / Collect

O God, who created us in your image, grant us the wisdom
and courage to share your loving kindness with others rather
than seeking our own aggrandizement; through Jesus Christ
our Savior. Amen.

OR

O God, who created us to be in communion with you and in
service to each other, grant that we will not be satisfied with
our lives until we are doing both faithfully; through Jesus
Christ our Savior. Amen.

OR

We enter your presence that we might offer our worship and
praise to you, our God and our redeemer, and so that we
might be strengthened and encouraged in our service to others. Amen.

Prayer of Confession

Leader: Let us confess to God and before one another our
sins and especially the way we seek our good above the good
of others.

People: We confess to you, O God, and before one another that we have sinned. We have allowed ourselves to be drawn to the false light of looking good in the eyes of others instead of to the true light of being of service to others. We often are more concerned about how the things we do look to others than about what good we could do for others. Forgive us our foolish ways and draw us back to the side of Jesus who has shown us how to offer self for others. Amen.

Leader: God seeks us and desires to heal us and then through us to heal all of creation. God welcomes your confession and offers you the power of the Spirit to amend your life.

Prayers of the People (and the Lord's Prayer)

We worship and adore you, O God, for your loving kindness and compassion are forever. Your love for your creation knows no bounds.

(The following paragraph may be used if a separate prayer of confession has not been used.)

We confess to you, O God, and before one another that we have sinned. We have allowed ourselves to be drawn to the false light of looking good in the eyes of others instead of to the true light of being of service to others. We often are more concerned about how the things we do look to others than about what good we could do for others. Forgive us our foolish ways and draw us back to the side of Jesus who has shown us how to offer self for others.

We give you thanks for all your kindness toward us and all of your creation. We thank you for the countless ways you have come to us and called us to life in its fullness.

(Other thanksgivings may be offered.)

We pray to you for our sisters and brothers in need, asking as you are about the work of healing their hurts that our prayers, our spirits, and our love might be a part of your ministry. Help us also to seek those ways in which we can be your physical presence to those who are hurting.

(Other intercessions may be offered.)
All these things we ask in the name of our Savior Jesus Christ, who taught us to pray together, saying:
Our Father... Amen.

(Or if the Lord's Prayer is not used at this point in the service)
All this we ask in the name of the Blessed and Holy Trinity. Amen.

Proper 18
Pentecost 16
Ordinary Time 23

Jeremiah 18:1-11
Philemon 1-21
Luke 14:25-33

Call to Worship
Leader: O God, you search us and know us.
People: You discern our thoughts from far away.
Leader: You search out our paths.
People: You are acquainted with all our ways.
Leader: How weighty to me are your thoughts, O God!
People: How vast is the sum of them!

OR

Leader: Come, let us count the cost of our discipleship.
People: Cost? We thought grace was free.
Leader: Grace is free. Discipleship is expensive!
People: Will it cost us friends? Money? Position?
Leader: It will cost us everything — but it gives us life, eternal and abundant.
People: It is a dear price but a dearer reward.

Hymns and Sacred Songs
"All Creatures of Our God and King"
found in:
UMH: 62   NCH: 17
H82: 400   CH: 22
PH: 455   LBW: 522

AAHH: 147　　　　　　　Renew: 47
NNBH: 33

"I Sing the Almighty Power of God"
found in:
UMH: 152　　　　　　　NCH: 12
H82: 398　　　　　　　 Renew: 54
PH: 288

"I Surrender All"
found in:
UMH: 354　　　　　　　NNBH: 198
AAHH: 396

"Pues Si Vivimos" ("When We Are Living")
found in:
UMH: 356　　　　　　　NCH: 499
PH: 400　　　　　　　　CH: 536

"Take My Life and Let It Be"
found in:
UMH: 399　　　　　　　NCH: 448
H82: 707　　　　　　　 CH: 609
PH: 391　　　　　　　　LBW: 406
NNBH: 213

"Seek Ye First"
found in:
UMH: 405　　　　　　　CH: 354
H82: 711　　　　　　　 CCB: 76
PH: 333

"Must Jesus Bear the Cross Alone"
found in:

UMH: 424
AAHH: 554

NNBH: 221

"Hope of the World"
found in:
UMH: 178
H82: 472
PH: 360

NCH: 46
CH: 538
LBW: 493

"Refiner's Fire"
found in:
CCB: 79

"God, You Are My God"
found in:
CCB: 60

Prayer for the Day / Collect

O God, who knows our hearts and minds better than we know ourselves, grant us the wisdom to know that only by making you and your way first in our lives and hearts can we ever truly love; through Jesus Christ our Savior. Amen.

OR

We have come to worship you, O God, because you are the one who knows us better than we know ourselves. You know how difficult it is for us to love and how difficult it is for us to choose wisely. As we listen for your word to us this day, help us to put all things we love into your hands so that we can let go of them. Amen.

Prayer of Confession

Leader: Let us confess to God and before one another our sins and especially our disordered affections.

People: We confess to you, O God, and before one another that we have sinned. We have clung to things we love so tightly that we have risked smothering them. We have failed to trust you enough to turn them loose into your loving hands. We have tried to be God and run the world around us. Forgive us our foolishness and shortsightedness that we may truly love you and trust that your love is enough for those we love. Free us to free them so that your reign may be more complete in them and us. Amen.

Leader: God's love is, indeed, great enough for us and for all that we care about. As God forgives us, God also empowers us to live in the freedom of love.

Prayers of the People (and the Lord's Prayer)
We worship and adore you, O God, the Creator and the knower of all things. There is nothing hidden from you and your love.

(The following paragraph may be used if a separate prayer of confession has not been used.)
We confess to you, O God, and before one another that we have sinned. We have clung to things we love so tightly that we have risked smothering them. We have failed to trust you enough to turn them loose into your loving hands. We have tried to be God and run the world around us. Forgive us our foolishness and shortsightedness that we may truly love you and trust that your love is enough for those we love. Free us to free them so that your reign may be more complete in them and us.

We give you thanks for all the ways you have called us to love and to freedom. Most of all we thank you for Jesus, who has come to us and called us to a radical new life that frees us from our fears and worries and allows us to commit all our precious ones and treasured things into your care.

(Other thanksgivings may be offered.)
We pray to you for one another in our need and for all your children and all your creation. We know others are as bound as we have been, and we know how easy it is for us to slip back into our bondage. We pray that as we open ourselves more completely to your love and grace we may find ourselves more open to sharing you with others through our words and our actions.

(Other intercessions may be offered.)
All these things we ask in the name of our Savior Jesus Christ, who taught us to pray together, saying:
Our Father... Amen.

(Or if the Lord's Prayer is not used at this point in the service)
All this we ask in the name of the Blessed and Holy Trinity. Amen.

Proper 19
Pentecost 17
Ordinary Time 24

Jeremiah 4:11-12, 22-28
1 Timothy 1:12-17
Luke 15:1-10

Call to Worship
Leader: God looks down from heaven on humankind
People: to see if there are any who are wise, who seek after God.
Leader: We have all gone astray, we are all alike perverse;
People: there is no one who does good, no, not one.
Leader: When the Lord restores the fortunes of his people,
People: Jacob will rejoice; Israel will be glad.

OR

Leader: The God of faithfulness calls into the holy presence.
People: We come to rest in the faithfulness of God.
Leader: God calls us to care for one another with steadfast love.
People: We offer to our sisters and brothers God's own love.
Leader: God calls us to reach out with the love to the stranger and our enemy.
People: By the grace of God, we will be faithful in loving those who are different from us and who are against us.

Hymns and Sacred Songs

"All People Who on Earth Do Dwell"
found in:

UMH: 75	NCH: 7
H82: 377/378	CH: 18
PH: 220/221	LBW: 245
NNBH: 36	

"Great Is Thy Faithfulness"
found in:

UMH: 140	NCH: 423
AAHH: 158	CH: 86
NNBH: 45	Renew: 249

"We Believe in One True God"
found in:
UMH: 85

"O Jesus, I Have Promised"
found in:

UMH: 396	NCH: 493
H82: 655	CH: 612
PH: 388/389	LBW: 503

"Take My Life and Let It Be"
found in:

UMH: 399	NCH: 448
H82: 707	CH: 609
PH: 391	LBW: 406
NNBH: 213	Renew: 150

"A Charge to Keep I Have"
found in:

UMH: 413	NNBH: 436
AAHH: 467/468	

"Dear Jesus, in Whose Life I See"
found in:
UMH: 468

"Stand Up, Stand Up for Jesus"
found in:
UMH: 514   NNBH: 409
H82: 561   CH: 613
AAHH: 476   LBW: 389

"The Steadfast Love of the Lord"
found in:
CCB: 28   Renew: 23

"I Call You Faithful"
found in:
CCB: 70

Prayer for the Day / Collect
O God, who is faithful in all things, grant that we may truly reflect your image in our faithfulness to you and your reign; through Jesus Christ our Savior. Amen.

OR

We come into your presence, faithful one, to worship you and to learn how to live in your reign. So fill us with your Spirit this day that we may find ourselves truly faithful to you and your Son, our Savior, Jesus Christ. Amen.

Prayer of Confession
Leader: Let us confess to God and before one another our sins and especially our lack of faithfulness to the God we have pledged to worship and serve.

People: We confess to you, O God, and before one another that we have sinned. We have offered ourselves to you and your reign, but we are so easily persuaded to follow other ways. We say Jesus is our Savior, but when we encounter the places where we are called to live in his way, we falter and look for a detour. Forgive us and redirect us so that we may truly be your faithful people. Amen.

Leader: God is faithful and welcomes us back when we have strayed away yet again. Live in the faithful presence of God's Spirit.

Prayers of the People (and the Lord's Prayer)

We worship you, O faithful God, because you do not turn from side to side but walk the straight and difficult path of love. When all else fails us in life, we know that you are faithful and gracious to your creation.

(The following paragraph may be used if a separate prayer of confession has not been used.)

We confess to you, O God, and before one another that we have sinned. We have offered ourselves to you and your reign, but we are so easily persuaded to follow other ways. We say Jesus is our Savior, but when we encounter the places where we are called to live in his way, we falter and look for a detour. Forgive us and redirect us so that we may truly be your faithful people.

We give you thanks for all the ways we experience your faithfulness and loving kindness toward us and all creation. We thank you for the rhythms of nature and life that reflect your steadfastness. We thank you for your presence that always surrounds us, though we are often unaware of you.

(Other thanksgivings may be offered.)
We pray for those who have not found safety and security in life and do not know your faithfulness. We pray that we may be the visible presence of your faithfulness to them.

(Other intercessions may be offered.)
All these things we ask in the name of our Savior Jesus Christ, who taught us to pray together, saying:
Our Father... Amen.

(Or if the Lord's Prayer is not used at this point in the service)
All this we ask in the name of the Blessed and Holy Trinity. Amen.

Proper 20
Pentecost 18
Ordinary Time 25

Jeremiah 8:18—9:1
1 Timothy 2:1-7
Luke 16:1-13

Call to Worship
Leader: God calls us to worship.
People: We come to bring our praises to God.
Leader: God calls us to responsibility.
People: We come to learn from our faithful God.
Leader: God calls us to responsibility in all our lives.
People: As God's image, we will strive to be responsible.

Hymns and Sacred Songs
"Holy, Holy, Holy! Lord God Almighty"
found in:

UMH: 64	NCH: 277
H82: 362	CH: 4
PH: 138	LBW: 165
AAHH: 329	Renew: 204
NNBH: 1	

"O God, Our Help in Ages Past"
found in:

UMH: 117	NCH: 25
H82: 680	CH: 67
AAHH: 170	LBW: 320
NNBH: 46	

"O Master, Let Me Walk with Thee"
found in:
UMH: 430   NCH: 503
H82: 659/660   CH: 602
PH: 357   LBW: 492
NNBH: 445

"Make Me a Captive, Lord"
found in:
UMH: 421   PH: 378

"Trust and Obey"
found in:
UMH: 467   NNBH: 322
AAHH: 380   CH: 556

"O Zion, Haste"
found in:
UMH: 573   NNBH: 422
H82: 539   LBW: 397

"How Shall They Hear the Word of God"
found in:
UMH: 649

"I Want to Be Ready"
found in:
UMH: 722   NCH: 616

"God, You Are My God"
found in:
CCB: 60

"Open Our Eyes, Lord"
found in:

"Find Us Faithful" by Steve Green

Prayer for the Day / Collect
O God, who is always faithful, grant us the grace to truly reflect your image by making us responsible in all our actions; through Jesus Christ our Savior. Amen.

OR

We come into your presence, O God, and celebrate your great faithfulness to us and to all your creation. As your Spirit fills us during this time of worship, may we be empowered to act with responsibility so that we reflect your image more clearly. Amen.

Prayer of Confession
Leader: Let us confess to God and before one another our sins and especially the way our irresponsibility dulls our reflection of God's faithfulness.
People: We confess to you, O God, and before one another that we have sinned. You have given your good creation for us to watch over as your stewards, and we have misused it for our own selfish purposes. We have polluted the air, the water, and the ground of your good earth. We have poisoned the earth and ourselves. You have given us the gift of community, but we have sinned against one another and divided the peoples of the earth into armed camps. We have not been reflections of your faithfulness but have instead been reflections of our own irresponsibility. Forgive us and call us once more to being your responsible people who truly reflect your faithfulness. Amen.

Leader: God is faithful and with joy welcomes you to once again take your place as his responsible stewards of creation and of each other.

Prayers of the People (and the Lord's Prayer)
We worship and adore you, our faithful God, for you are the rock of ages who shelters us and preserves us.

(The following paragraph may be used if a separate prayer of confession has not been used.)
We confess to you, O God, and before one another that we have sinned. You have given your good creation for us to watch over as your stewards, and we have misused it for our own selfish purposes. We have polluted the air, the water, and the ground of your good earth. We have poisoned the earth and ourselves. You have given us the gift of community, but we have sinned against one another and divided the peoples of the earth into armed camps. We have not been reflections of your faithfulness but have instead been reflections of our own irresponsibility. Forgive us and call us once more to being your responsible people who truly reflect your faithfulness.

We offer our thanksgivings to you for all the ways you have acted in faithful caring toward us. We thank you for your Spirit that dwells within us and among us, calling us to wholeness and you. We thank you for those who have been responsible in their dealings with us so that we learned about your faithfulness.

(Other thanksgivings may be offered.)
We pray for each other and for all your creation. We pray for those who have not found the world. And we pray for those to be responsible co-habitants of this earth. Many have suffered from violence and abuse; many have been deserted

and forsaken. As you move among them, may our love and care be part of your healing presence.

(Other intercessions may be offered.)
All these things we ask in the name of our Savior Jesus Christ, who taught us to pray together, saying:
Our Father... Amen.

(Or if the Lord's Prayer is not used at this point in the service)
All this we ask in the name of the Blessed and Holy Trinity. Amen.

Proper 21
Pentecost 19
Ordinary Time 26

Jeremiah 32:1-3a, 6-15
1 Timothy 6:6-19
Luke 16:19-31

Call to Worship
Leader: You who live in the shelter of the most high,
People: who abide in the shadow of the almighty,
Leader: will say to God, "My refuge and my fortress;
People: my God, in whom I trust."
Leader: For God will cover you and under God's wings you
will find refuge;
People: God's faithfulness is a shield and buckler.

OR

Leader: Come and stand in the presence of our God.
People: We come to rejoice in God's love for us.
Leader: Come and stand in solidarity with all God's chil-
dren.
People: With ALL God's children?
Leader: "For God so loved the WORLD...."
People: We stand with God and with all God's children.

Hymns and Sacred Songs
"Sing Praise to God Who Reigns Above"
found in:

UMH: 126	NCH: 6
H82: 408	CH: 6
PH: 483	

"O God, Our Help in Ages Past"
found in:
UMH: 117
H82: 680
AAHH: 170
NNBH: 46

NCH: 25
CH: 67
LBW: 320
ELW: 632

"A Mighty Fortress Is Our God"
found in:
UMH: 110
H82: 687/688
PH: 260
AAHH: 124
NNBH: 37

NCH: 439/440
CH: 65
LBW: 228/229
ELW: 503/504/505

"Jesu, Jesu"
found in:
UMH: 432
H82: 602
PH: 367

NCH: 498
CH: 600
ELW: 708

"Cuando El Pobre" ("When the Poor Ones")
found in:
UMH: 434
PH: 407

CH: 662
ELW: 725

"O God of Every Nation"
found in:
UMH: 435
H82: 607
PH: 289

CH: 680
LBW: 416
ELW: 713

"What Does the Lord Require"
found in:
UMH: 441

PH: 405

H82: 605 CH: 659

"O God Who Shaped Creation"
found in:
UMH: 443

"On Eagle's Wings"
found in:
CCB: 97   CH: 77
Renew: 112   ELW: 787
UMH: 143

"Make Me a Servant"
found in:
CCB: 90

Prayer for the Day / Collect
O God, who loves all your creation, give us the grace to see
that your love is for all, even those we might look down on
or despise; through Jesus Christ our Savior. Amen.

OR

We come to worship you, O God, not because we are worthy
but because you call us. We know that we are the least of your
creatures, and we rejoice that you invite even us into your
presence. Help us as we hear your good news that we might
see those around us as beloved as you see them. Amen.

Prayer of Confession
Leader: Let us confess to God and before one another our
sins and especially our quickness to judge others as less worthy than ourselves.
**People: We confess to you, O God, and before one an-
other that we have sinned. We have looked at our sisters**

245

and brothers and have judged them to be less than we are. We would gladly let them take care of our needs but we have little thought for theirs. We gladly reduce their tip if they do not take care of our smallest desire; yet we never consider what it costs them to live near enough to be able to serve us. Forgive us our judging and condemning ways and open our eyes to see others as your beloved children. Amen.

Leader: God is always ready to help us move from judgment to acceptance. Receive God's forgiveness and share that grace with those around you.

Prayers of the People (and the Lord's Prayer)

We worship and give you praise, O God, for the love that moved you to make creation. We praise you for the wonder of being your children.

(The following paragraph may be used if a separate prayer of confession has not been used.)

We confess to you, O God, and before one another that we have sinned. We have looked at our sisters and brothers and have judged them to be less than we are. We would gladly let them take care of our needs but we have little thought for theirs. We gladly reduce their tip if they do not take care of our smallest desire; yet we never consider what it costs them to live near enough to be able to serve us. Forgive us our judging and condemning ways and open our eyes to see others as your beloved children.

We give you thanks for all the ways in which you have shown your love for us. You have created us and given us all the wonders and splendors of creation to enjoy and to care for in your name. You have blessed us with your Spirit and have come among us as the Christ.

(Other thanksgivings may be offered.)

246

We pray for those who are judged and condemned so readily by others. We pray for those who are deemed less acceptable because of their looks, their social status, or their poverty. We pray for those rejected because of the color of their skin or the makeup of the psyche. We pray for ourselves, as your people, your image, that we may be more like Jesus in accepting others.

(Other intercessions may be offered.)
All these things we ask in the name of our Savior Jesus Christ, who taught us to pray together, saying:
Our Father... Amen.

(Or if the Lord's Prayer is not used at this point in the service)
All this we ask in the name of the Blessed and Holy Trinity. Amen.

Proper 22
Pentecost 20
Ordinary Time 27

Lamentations 1:1-6
2 Timothy 1:1-14
Luke 17:5-10

Call to Worship
Leader: By the rivers of Babylon — there we sat down
People: and there we wept when we remembered Zion.
Leader: On the willows there we hung up our harps.
People: For there our captors asked us for songs,
Leader: and our tormentors asked for mirth,
People: saying, "Sing us one of the songs of Zion!"

OR

Leader: Come and join with the one who is the Christ of God.
People: We come to worship and adore the Christ.
Leader: Come and kneel with him before the poor.
People: Why isn't he seated on a throne?
Leader: He has come to serve and to save.
People: Make us servants that we may serve with Christ.

Hymns and Sacred Songs
"My Jesus, I Love Thee"
found in:
UMH: 17
AAHH: 574
NNBH: 39

CH: 349
Renew: 275

"When in Our Music God Is Glorified"
found in:
UMH: 68
H82: 420
PH: 264
AAHH: 112
NCH: 561

CH: 7
LBW: 555
ELW: 850/851
Renew: 62

"O Love Divine, What Hast Thou Done"
found in:
UMH: 287

"What Wondrous Love Is This"
found in:
UMH: 292
H82: 439
PH: 85
NCH: 223

CH: 200
LBW: 385
ELW: 666
Renew: 277

"Jesu, Jesu"
found in:
UMH: 432
H82: 602
PH: 367
NCH: 498

CH: 600
ELW: 708
Renew: 289

"Am I a Soldier of the Cross"
found in:
UMH: 511
AAHH: 482/483/603

NNBH: 259

"Are Ye Able"
found in:
UMH: 530
NNBH: 223

CH: 621

"Where Charity and Love Prevail"
found in:
UMH: 549   LBW: 126
H82: 581   ELW: 359
NCH: 396

"Make Me a Servant"
found in:
CCB: 90

"We Are His Hands"
found in:
CCB: 85

Prayer for the Day / Collect

O God, who came among us in the form of a slave, give us the grace to accept our position of servant so that others may enter into your eternal reign; through Jesus Christ our Savior. Amen.

OR

We come to worship you, O God, as the Creator of all that was, that is, and that is to come. Yet we know you also as the one who comes in the form of a slave to give yourself to your creation. Help us this day to lay aside our pretenses and to take on the role of servant to others. Amen.

Prayer of Confession

Leader: Let us confess to God and before one another our sins and especially our reluctance to serve and our eagerness to be served.

People: We confess to you, O God, and before one another that we have sinned. We claim to be followers of Jesus who came among us to serve and yet we insist on being

served. **We think being Christian gives us a special status instead of it being the mark of servanthood. Forgive us our selfishness and call us once again to follow Jesus by taking up his basin and towel to serve others. Amen.**
Leader: Jesus came to bring us life even if it meant he had to kneel to serve. Forgiveness is freely given as are the basin and towel.

Prayers of the People (and the Lord's Prayer)
Blessing, power, and majesty are yours, O God, and yet you came to your creation as a slave. You take on the role of servant and seek only our good.

(The following paragraph may be used if a separate prayer of confession has not been used.)
We confess to you, O God, and before one another that we have sinned. We claim to be followers of Jesus who came among us to serve and yet we insist on being served. We think being Christian gives us a special status instead of it being the mark of servanthood. Forgive us our selfishness and call us once again to follow Jesus by taking up his basin and towel to serve others.

We give you thanks for all the ways you have shown your love for us. We thank you for the example of Jesus who knelt at the feet of his disciples and acted as their servant to teach us the way to live through serving others.

(Other thanksgivings may be offered.)
We pray for those who do not have an opportunity to take on a life of service because they are forced into it. We pray for those who are forced into slavery and submission by others or by circumstances.

(Other intercessions may be offered.)

251

All these things we ask in the name of our Savior Jesus Christ, who taught us to pray together, saying:
Our Father... Amen.

(Or if the Lord's Prayer is not used at this point in the service)
All this we ask in the name of the Blessed and Holy Trinity. Amen.

Proper 23
Pentecost 21
Ordinary Time 28

Jeremiah 29:1, 4-7
2 Timothy 2:8-15
Luke 17:11-19

Call to Worship
Leader: Make a joyful noise to our God!
People: Let us sing glory to the name of God.
Leader: Let all the earth worship God.
People: God's deeds are indeed awesome.
Leader: Come and celebrate all God has done.
People: God's deeds are wonderful beyond description!

OR

Leader: Come and worship the God who never forsakes us.
People: Is God with us in these times of distress?
Leader: God is with us in all our troubles and afflictions.
People: But we are in war, economic trouble, and despair.
Leader: God knows who we are and where we are.
People: We celebrate the God who never leaves us.

Hymns and Sacred Songs
"How Firm a Foundation"
found in:
UMH: 529
H82: 636/637
PH: 361
AAHH: 146

NNBH: 48
NCH: 407
CH: 618
LBW: 507

"Jesus, Savior, Pilot Me"
found in:
UMH: 509   NCH: 441
NNBH: 243   LBW: 334

"Come, Ye Disconsolate"
found in:
UMH: 510   NNBH: 264
AAHH: 421   CH: 502

"O God, Our Help in Ages Past"
found in:
UMH: 117   NCH: 25
H82: 680   CH: 67
AAHH: 170   LBW: 320
NNBH: 46

"O Thou, in Whose Presence"
found in:
UMH: 518

"Be Still, My Soul"
found in:
UMH: 534   NCH: 488
AAHH: 135   CH: 566
NNBH: 263

"We Shall Overcome"
found in:
UMH: 533   NCH: 570
AAHH: 542   CH: 630
NNBH: 501

"Jesus, Priceless Treasure"
found in:

UMH: 532
PH: 365
NNBH: 74

NCH: 480
LBW: 457/458

"All I Need Is You"
found in:
CCB: 100

"Cares Chorus"
found in:
CCB: 53

Prayer for the Day / Collect
O God, who continues to work with your creatures no matter how far they stray from your path, grant us the faithfulness to continue to walk with you and build your reign with what we have; through Jesus Christ our Savior. Amen.

OR

We come to worship you, O God, and to implore you to strengthen us that we might be able to live faithfully as disciples of Jesus in these times and these places. Amen.

Prayer of Confession
Leader: Let us confess to God and before one another our sins and especially the way we complain about how things are instead of making them better.
People: We confess to you, O God, and before one another that we have sinned. We have looked around at our circumstances and want nothing more than for you to change things for us. We whine and complain that things are not as we want them to be. We forget that creation is not what you desire it to be either. Forgive us our foolish, self-centered ways and empower us to live faithfully in

255

the circumstances we find ourselves in so that we may enable your reign to come in its fullness. Amen.

Leader: God is always willing to work with us where we are and to help us become the people we need to become. Receive the power of the risen Christ and live as his disciples this day and always.

Prayers of the People (and the Lord's Prayer)

O God, who created and is ever creating, we worship you for your faithfulness to your creation and to us, your creatures. You made us in your image and have remained our faithful God.

(The following paragraph may be used if a separate prayer of confession has not been used.)

We confess to you, O God, and before one another that we have sinned. We have looked around at our circumstances and want nothing more than for you to change things for us. We whine and complain that things are not as we want them to be. We forget that creation is not what you desire it to be either. Forgive us our foolish, self-centered ways and empower us to live faithfully in the circumstances we find ourselves in so that we may enable your reign to come in its fullness.

We give you thanks for all the times when you have not given up on us. When we have chosen foolishly, blindly, or willfully, you have stayed with us, wooing us back into your path of life and wholeness.

(Other thanksgivings may be offered.)

We pray for all who are in need and particularly for those who are in circumstances that seem insurmountable. We pray that your Spirit might lift them up and energize them with the hope of finding a way in their wilderness.

(Other intercessions may be offered.)
All these things we ask in the name of our Savior Jesus
Christ, who taught us to pray together, saying:
Our Father... Amen.

(Or if the Lord's Prayer is not used at this point in the ser-vice)
All this we ask in the name of the Blessed and Holy Trinity.
Amen.

Proper 24
Pentecost 22
Ordinary Time 29

Jeremiah 31:27-34
2 Timothy 3:14—4:5
Luke 18:1-8

Call to Worship
Leader: Oh, how lovely is God's way!
People: It is our meditation all day long.
Leader: How sweet are God's words!
People: They are sweeter than honey in our mouths.
Leader: God's teaching gives understanding.
People: Therefore we do not walk in the way that is false.

OR

Leader: Come and learn from God the way of life.
People: We come seeking life, abundant and full.
Leader: God's ways are sweet and dear to the heart.
People: We will commit God's way to our soul.
Leader: God receives all those who seek life in him.
People: In God alone is our true life.

Hymns and Sacred Songs
"All People that on Earth Do Dwell"
found in:

UMH: 75	NCH: 7
H82: 377/378	CH: 18
PH: 220/221	LBW: 245
NNBH: 36	

"The God of Abraham Praise"
found in:
UMH: 116   LBW: 51
H82: 401   Renew: 24
CH: 544

"We Believe in One True God"
found in:
UMH: 85

"Let Us Plead for Faith Alone"
found in:
UMH: 385

"When Our Confidence Is Shaken"
found in:
UMH: 505   CH: 534

"How Firm a Foundation"
found in:
UMH: 529   NNBH: 48
H82: 636/637   NCH: 407
PH: 361   CH: 618
AAHH: 146   LBW: 507

"The Church's One Foundation"
found in:
UMH: 545/546   NNBH: 297
H82: 525   NCH: 386
PH: 442   CH: 272
AAHH: 337   LBW: 365

"Break Thou the Bread of Life"
found in:
UMH: 599   NCH: 321

PH: 329
AAHH: 334
NNBH: 295

CH: 321
LBW: 235

"Thy Word Is a Lamp"
found in:
UMH: 601

Renew: 94

"Open Our Eyes, Lord"
found in:
CCB: 77

Renew: 91

"We Believe (in God the Father)"
found in:
Renew: 156

"We Believe in God Almighty"
found in:
Renew: 157

Prayer for the Day / Collect
O God, whose great desire is to bring abundant life to your children, grant us the wisdom to learn from you and to follow your path; through Jesus Christ our Savior. Amen.

OR

We come to worship you, the God who created us, and to learn from you the true way we need to follow to find abundant life. Open our hearts and minds to the power of your Spirit that we may learn from you and follow you all our days. Amen.

Prayer of Confession

Leader: Let us confess to God and before one another our sins and especially the ways in which we make up our own rules for life.

People: We confess to you, O God, and before one another that we have sinned. We have used your counsel and direction for our own gain and not to reach you and the abundant life you desire for us. We have taken your counsels that suit us and prop up our own views and ignored the rest. We have not been good students, but have, in sloth, taken the easy way. Forgive us and renew us in your Spirit that we might better learn of you and your ways and allow them to transform us into your image. Amen.

Leader: God is the loving one who gave us life and the way of life. God delights when we turn and return to our senses. Come and learn of God that you may have life eternal.

Prayers of the People (and the Lord's Prayer)

We come to worship and adore the God who gives us life and the way that leads to life eternal.

(The following paragraph may be used if a separate prayer of confession has not been used.)

We confess to you, O God, and before one another that we have sinned. We have used your counsel and direction for our own gain and not to reach you and the abundant life you desire for us. We have taken your counsels that suit us and prop up our own views and ignored the rest. We have not been good students, but have, in sloth, taken the easy way. Forgive us and renew us in your Spirit that we might better learn of you and your ways and allow them to transform us into your image.

We give you thanks for all the ways in which you have brought life, abundant and joyful, to us. You have loved us and cared for us in ways that are evident to us and in many other ways that we have not noticed. We thank you most of all for Jesus, who comes to lead us to you and to life eternal.

(Other thanksgivings may be offered.)
We offer to you the world that you love and care for. As you watch over it and long to draw your creatures to you, help us to be part of that love that draws people to life. We are painfully aware of the many ways your creatures ignore your call and head to death. May your love draw them, at last, to you and to your life.

(Other intercessions may be offered.)
All these things we ask in the name of our Savior Jesus Christ, who taught us to pray together, saying:
Our Father... Amen.

(Or if the Lord's Prayer is not used at this point in the service)
All this we ask in the name of the Blessed and Holy Trinity. Amen.

Proper 25
Pentecost 23
Ordinary Time 30

Joel 2:23-32
2 Timothy 4:6-8, 16-18
Luke 18:9-14

Call to Worship
Leader: Praise is due to you, O God, in Zion;
People: and to you shall vows be performed.
Leader: When deeds of iniquity overwhelm us,
People: you forgive our transgressions.
Leader: Happy are those whom you choose.
People: We shall be satisfied with the goodness of your house.

OR

Leader: Come and worship God, the Holy One.
People: But we are a sinful people.
Leader: God knows who you are and the condition of your lives.
People: Then God knows we are sinful through and through.
Leader: God knows you, loves you, and accepts you as you are.
People: With relief and gratitude we come into God's presence.

Hymns and Sacred Songs
"Holy, Holy, Holy! Lord God Almighty"
found in:

UMH: 64
H82: 362
PH: 138
AAHH: 329
NNBH: 1

NCH: 277
CH: 4
LBW: 165
Renew: 204

"Holy God, We Praise Thy Name"
found in:
UMH: 79
H82: 366
PH: 460

NNBH: 13
NCH: 276
LBW: 535

"Just As I Am, Without One Plea"
found in:
UMH: 357
H82: 693
PH: 370
AAHH: 344/345
NNBH: 167

NCH: 207
CH: 339
LBW: 296
Renew: 140

"It's Me, It's Me, O Lord"
found in:
UMH: 352
NNBH: 496

CH: 579

"Come, Ye Sinners, Poor and Needy"
found in:
UMH: 340

"Lift High the Cross"
found in:
UMH: 159
H82: 473
PH: 371
AAHH: 242

NCH: 198
CH: 108
LBW: 377
Renew: 297

"Christ, Whose Glory Fills the Skies"
found in:
UMH: 173   PH: 462/463
H82: 6/7   LBW: 265

"Breathe on Me, Breath of God"
found in:
UMH: 420   NNBH: 126
H82: 508   NCH: 292
PH: 316   CH: 254
AAHH: 317   LBW: 488

"People Need the Lord"
found in:
CCB: 52

"All I Need Is You"
found in:
CCB: 100

Prayer for the Day / Collect

O God, who knows us better than we could ever know ourselves, grant us the courage to come to you as we are so that we can leave more like you; through Jesus Christ our Savior. Amen.

OR

We come into your presence, holy God, knowing that we are a sinful people and that we dwell in a world of sinfulness. We come not because we are worthy but because you call us in love. Draw us into the power of your Spirit that we may be transformed and empowered to live as your children. Amen.

Prayer of Confession

Leader: Let us confess to God and before one another our sins and especially the ways we have submitted to our tendency for selfishness and sinful behavior.

People: **We confess to you, O God, and before one another that we have sinned. We live in a sinful world, and we have chosen to participate in its sinfulness. We have indulged our selfish ambitions, and we have shunned your way of life through dying to that selfishness. We have seen and tasted the goodness of the Promised Land, and yet we long for the fleshpots of Egypt. Forgive us and so fill us with your Spirit that we may truly follow Jesus and become your loving children.**

Leader: God knows our weakness and our sinfulness. God receives us as we are and gives us his own Spirit that we may become more like our Savior, Jesus.

Prayers of the People (and the Lord's Prayer)

We praise your name, O Holy One, who sits enthroned above all. Your holiness is pure and your nature is love. You never deviate or change from who you are.

(The following paragraph may be used if a separate prayer of confession has not been used.)

We confess to you, O God, and before one another that we have sinned. We live in a sinful world, and we have chosen to participate in its sinfulness. We have indulged our selfish ambitions, and we have shunned your way of life through dying to that selfishness. We have seen and tasted the goodness of the Promised Land, and yet we long for the fleshpots of Egypt. Forgive us and so fill us with your Spirit that we may truly follow Jesus and become your loving children.

We give you thanks for all the blessings we have received from you. We thank you for the ways in which you lead us and shepherd us toward a life that is abundant and eternal.

You call us your children, and you teach us the ways of life and truth. We thank you for Jesus, who shows us that we are both loved as we are and empowered to become like you.

(Other thanksgivings may be offered.)
We pray for ourselves and our sinful world. We have been so selfish that we have all but destroyed your people and your earth. Everywhere we look we see people in need and often it is because of what we are doing to each other. As you work for wholeness, empower us to join in your work of salvation.

(Other intercessions may be offered.)
All these things we ask in the name of our Savior Jesus Christ, who taught us to pray together, saying:
Our Father... Amen.

(Or if the Lord's Prayer is not used at this point in the service)
All this we ask in the name of the Blessed and Holy Trinity. Amen.

Reformation Day

Jeremiah 31:31-34
Romans 3:19-28
John 8:31-36

Call to Worship
Leader: God is our refuge and our strength.
People: God is a very present help in time of trouble.
Leader: We will not fear even if the earth changes.
People: We will not fear though the mountains shake.
Leader: The God of hosts is with us.
People: The God of Jacob is our refuge.

OR

Leader: Come and draw near to God.
People: We come with fear for we are not what we ought to be.
Leader: God already knows that and desires to transform our lives and reform our community.
People: We know we need to change. We trust in God's loving counsel.
Leader: Draw near to God and learn the truth.
People: We seek the truth for it will set us free.

Hymns and Sacred Songs
"A Mighty Fortress"
found in:
UMH: 110
H82: 687/688
PH: 200
AAHH: 124

NNBH: 374
NCH: 439/440
CH: 65
LBW: 228/229

"O Church of God, United"
found in:
UMH: 547

"The Church's One Foundation"
found in:
UMH: 545/546   NNBH: 297
H82: 525   NCH: 386
PH: 442   CH: 272
AAHH: 337   LBW: 369

"Forward Through the Ages"
found in:
UMH: 555   NCH: 377

"We Are the Church"
found in:
UMH: 558

"God of Grace and God of Glory"
found in:
UMH: 577   CH: 464
H82: 594/595   LBW: 415
PH: 420   Renew: 301
NCH: 436

"When the Church of Jesus"
found in:
UMH: 592   CH: 470

"Christ Loves the Church"
found in:
UMH: 590

"Our God Reigns"
found in:
CCB: 33

"Holy Ground"
found in:
CCB: 5

Prayer for the Day / Collect
O God, who calls us into community, grant us the faith to trust you to help us reform our communities so that they may reflect your reign and your love; through Jesus Christ our Savior. Amen.

OR

You have called us, O God, into your presence so that we might offer you our worship as you offer us your guidance and salvation. Help us to be open to your love so that not only our individual lives but our very communities might be changed into your glory. Amen.

Prayer of Confession
Leader: Let us confess to God and before one another our sins and especially the ways we hang on to traditions that no longer work and deify our institutions.
People: We confess to you, O God, and before one another that we have sinned. There are things in our past that were helpful to us in knowing you and now we find that we cling to them as if they were what saved us and not you. Forgive us our foolishness and help us to open our lives to the fresh winds of your Spirit as you transform us and reform our institutions and communities. Amen.
Leader: God loves us and knows how difficult change can be for us. But God's love for us means that he wants us to grow

and to grow up. Receive the love and forgiveness of God that will change us and make us better.

Prayers of the People (and the Lord's Prayer)

We worship and praise your holy name, O God, for you are our Creator and redeemer. You constantly come to us to recreate us into your image.

(The following paragraph may be used if a separate prayer of confession has not been used.)
We confess to you, O God, and before one another that we have sinned. There are things in our past that were helpful to us in knowing you and now we find that we cling to them as if they were what saved us and not you. Forgive us our foolishness and help us to open our lives to the fresh winds of your Spirit as you transform us and reform our institutions and communities.

We give you thanks that you do not leave us alone to our own devices but come and offer us guidance and the very transformation of our beings. You will not rest until every person, every institution, every community has been reformed and brought into harmony with your reign.

(Other thanksgivings may be offered.)
We pray for ourselves and all creation as we are aware of how very far we are from your ideal for us. As you move among your creation seeking to redeem and claim each part, help us to not only offer ourselves for your reformation but to offer ourselves in helping others find the joy of living in your ways.

(Other intercessions may be offered.)
All these things we ask in the name of our Savior Jesus Christ, who taught us to pray together, saying:
Our Father....Amen.

271

(Or if the Our Father is not used at this point in the service)
All this we ask in the name of the Blessed and Holy Trinity.
Amen.

All Saints

Daniel 7:1-3, 15-18
Ephesians 1:11-23
Luke 6:20-31

Call to Worship
Leader: The earth is God's and all that is in it,
People: the world, and those who live in it;
Leader: for God has founded it on the seas
People: and established it on the rivers.
Leader: Who shall ascend the hill of God?
People: And who shall stand in God's holy place?
Leader: Those who have clean hands and pure hearts,
People: who do not lift up their souls to what is false and do not swear deceitfully.
Leader: They will receive blessing from God,
People: and vindication from the God of their salvation.

OR

Leader: Come into the presence of the God of us all.
People: We come to praise our God and give thanks for the saints.
Leader: Sing joyfully with those who have reached their prize.
People: We rejoice with those who have entered the church triumphant.
Leader: Let us welcome them and their witness into our midst.
People: Welcome all you saints. Let us praise God together.

Hymns and Sacred Songs

"For All the Saints"
found in:

UMH: 711	NCH: 299
H82: 287	CH: 637
PH: 526	LBW: 174
AAHH: 339	ELW: 422
NNBH: 301	

"I Sing a Song of the Saints of God"
found in:

UMH: 712	PH: 364
H82: 293	NCH: 295

"Rejoice in God's Saints"
found in:

UMH: 708	ELW: 418
CH: 476	

"Come, Let Us Join Our Friends Above"
found in:

UMH: 709	ELW: 847

"All Creatures of Our God and King"
found in:

UMH: 62	NCH: 17
H82: 400	CH: 22
PH: 455	LBW: 527
AAHH: 147	ELW: 835
NNBH: 33	Renew: 47

"When in Our Music God Is Glorified"
found in:

UMH: 68	NCH: 561
H82: 420	CH: 7

PH: 264   LBW: 555
AAHH: 112   ELW: 850/851

"A Mighty Fortress Is Our God"
found in:
UMH: 110   NCH: 439/440
H82: 687/688   CH: 65
PH: 260   LBW: 228/229
AAHH: 124   ELW: 503/504/505
NNBH: 37

"O God, Our Help in Ages Past"
found in:
UMH: 117   NCH: 25
H82: 680   CH: 67
AAHH: 170   LBW: 320
NNBH: 46   ELW: 632

"God, You Are My God"
found in:
CCB: 60

"Create in Me a Clean Heart"
found in:
CCB: 54   Renew: 181/182

Prayer for the Day / Collect
O God, who is the home of all the saints, grant us the courage to live our faith so that those who follow us will rise up
and call us blessed; through Jesus Christ our Savior. Amen.

OR

We come into your presence, O God, to praise you for the
saints you have called to serve you. We thank you for those

who have stood the test of martyrdom and those who have lived quiet, faithful lives. As we worship you, so fill us with your Spirit that we may be faithful for those who follow us. Amen.

Prayer of Confession

Leader: Let us confess to God and before one another our sins and especially the ways we forget that others are, have been, and will be part of your church.

People: We confess to you, O God, and before one another that we have sinned. We often think that we are the only ones who have every tried to follow Jesus. We act as if our struggles with sin and evil are different from the struggles of others. We think the insights we have about the faith are ours alone. We forget that generations have struggled and have left us a rich heritage to draw from. Forgive us and draw us closer to you that we may draw closer to all your saints. Amen.

Leader: God desires for all the saints to be gathered together. God welcomes us home.

Prayers of the People (and the Lord's Prayer)

We bend our knee before you, O God, who created us and have brought us into your new creation in Jesus Christ.

(The following paragraph may be used if a separate prayer of confessions has not been used.)

We confess to you, O God, and before one another that we have sinned. We often think that we are the only ones who have every tried to follow Jesus. We act as if our struggles with sin and evil are different from the struggles of others. We think the insights we have about the faith are ours alone. We forget that generations have struggled and have left us a rich heritage to draw from. Forgive us and draw us closer to you that we may draw closer to all your saints.

We give you thanks for all those who have gone before us in the faith. We thank you for their witness and the legacy of faith they have given us. We thank you for all those around the world who stand as our brothers and sisters in Christ. We thank you for the various ways they express their faith and teach us of the wideness of your love and grace.

(Other thanksgivings may be offered.)
We pray for those who will follow us in faith. We pray that we may be faithful so that they will learn of your faithfulness.

(Other intercessions may be offered.)
All these things we ask in the name of our Savior Jesus Christ, who taught us to pray together, saying:
Our Father... Amen.

(Or if the Lord's Prayer is not used at this point in the service.)
All this we ask in the name of the Blessed and Holy Trinity. Amen.

Proper 26
Pentecost 24
Ordinary Time 31

Habakkuk 1:1-4; 2:1-4
2 Thessalonians 1:1-4, 11-12
Luke 19:1-10

Call to Worship
Leader: You are righteous, O God, and your judgments are right.
People: You have spoken in righteousness and in all faithfulness.
Leader: Your promise is well-tried, and your servants love it.
People: Your righteousness is an everlasting righteousness.
Leader: Your law is the truth.
People: Give us understanding that we may live.

OR

Leader: Come, you sinners, to the God of grace.
People: God welcomes the sinner who repents.
Leader: God welcomes sinners before they repent.
People: What about God's justice?
Leader: God's justice is the salvation of all creation.
People: Even for those who don't deserve it?
Leader: Yes! Even for you and me!

Hymns and Sacred Songs
"Hope of the World"
found in:

UMH: 178   NCH: 46
H82: 472   CH: 538
PH: 360   LBW: 493

"Love Divine, All Loves Excelling"
found in:
UMH: 384   NCH: 43
H82: 657   CH: 517
PH: 376   LBW: 315
AAHH: 440   Renew: 196
NNBH: 65

"Come, Sinners, to the Gospel Feast"
found in:
UMH: 339

"Hallelujah! What a Savior"
found in:
UMH: 165

"Tu Has Venido a la Orilla" ("Lord, You Have Come to the Lakeshore")
found in:
UMH: 344   CH: 342
PH: 377

"It's Me, It's Me, O Lord"
found in:
UMH: 352   CH: 579
NNBH: 496

"I Stand Amazed in the Presence"
found in:
UMH: 371

"Amazing Grace"
found in:
UMH: 378
H82: 671
PH: 280
AAHH: 271/272
NNBH: 161/163

NCH: 547/548
CH: 546
LBW: 448
Renew: 189

"Your Loving Kindness Is Better than Life"
found in:
CCB: 26

"The Steadfast Love of the Lord"
found in:
CCB: 28

Renew: 23

Prayer for the Day / Collect

O God of extraordinary grace, grant us the eyes of faith that we may see that we all are held in the web of sin and need your redemption; through Jesus Christ our Savior. Amen.

OR

We come to rejoice in the abundance of God's grace, but we also know we are not as gracious as our God. Help us to hear you speak in this time of worship and to be transformed more into your image of gracious forgiveness for all. Amen.

Prayer of Confession

Leader: Let us confess to God and before one another our sins and especially the way we gladly receive grace but wish to withhold it from others.

People: We confess to you, O God, and before one another that we have sinned. We have accepted your grace for ourselves as if it were a reward we earned, as if we

deserved it. Yet we look at others and feel that they would only be eligible for your love if they turned their lives around and became more like us. We pat ourselves on the back because we have done the right thing and repented of our sins. But we have not really left them. We have done just enough that we feel you will take us to heaven. Forgive us our foolishness. Help us to realize we never would have been able to turn to you except that you came to us in grace. So fill us with the love and power of your Spirit that we may share your gracious love and forgiveness with all your children. Amen.

Leader: God is a gracious God and extends love, grace, and forgiveness to all, even us.

Prayers of the People (and the Lord's Prayer)
We worship and adore you, O God, because of your holiness. There is no duplicity in you but rather your love and your actions are one.

(The following paragraph may be used if a separate prayer of confession has not been used.)
We confess to you, O God, and before one another that we have sinned. We have accepted your grace for ourselves as if it were a reward we earned, as if we deserved it. Yet we look at others and feel that they would only be eligible for your love if they turned their lives around and became more like us. We pat ourselves on the back because we have done the right thing and repented of our sins. But we have not really left them. We have done just enough that we feel you will take us to heaven. Forgive us our foolishness. Help us to realize we never would have been able to turn to you except that you came to us in grace. So fill us with the love and power of your Spirit that we may share your gracious love and forgiveness with all your children.

281

We give you thanks for all the ways in which we have received your grace. When we are honest with ourselves, we know that we are as sinful as the next person and as undeserving of your love as anyone. Yet you love us and care for us in a multitude of ways and most of the time we are totally unaware of how you are at work in our lives.

(Other thanksgivings may be offered.)
Your gracious love has so surrounded us throughout our lives that it is in confidence that we offer to you those who are on our hearts. We know that you are already at work in their lives, calling them to wholeness and your love. May our love and spirits join yours in the gracious work of healing. Help us to put your love into the words and actions of our lives so that we can be part of your work of redemption.

(Other intercessions may be offered.)
All these things we ask in the name of our Savior Jesus Christ, who taught us to pray together, saying:
Our Father... Amen.

(Or if the Lord's Prayer is not used at this point in the service)
All this we ask in the name of the Blessed and Holy Trinity. Amen.

Proper 27
Pentecost 25
Ordinary Time 32

Haggai 1:15b—2:9
2 Thessalonians 2:1-5, 13-17
Luke 20:27-38

Call to Worship
Leader: God's ways are always just.
People: God's doings are always kind.
Leader: God is near to all who call.
People: God is near to all who call in truth.
Leader: Let us speak the praise of God.
People: Let us bless God's holy name forever and ever.

OR

Leader: Come and find the way.
People: We come seeking a path.
Leader: Come and find the truth.
People: We come bombarded with lies.
Leader: Come and find the life.
People: We come seeking a way from death.
Leader: Come and follow Jesus.
People: We come to follow our Savior Jesus.

Hymns and Sacred Songs
"Be Thou My Vision"
found in:

UMH: 451	NCH: 451
H82: 488	CH: 595
PH: 339	Renew: 151

"Come, My Way, My Truth, My Life"
found in:
UMH: 164   NCH: 331
H82: 487   LBW: 513

"Jesus Calls Us"
found in:
UMH: 398   NCH: 171/172
H82: 549/550   CH: 337
NNBH: 183   LBW: 494

"Lord, I Want to Be a Christian"
found in:
UMH: 402   NCH: 454
PH: 372   CH: 589
AAHH: 463   Renew: 145
NNBH: 156

"Dear Lord, Lead Me Day by Day"
found in:
UMH: 411

"O Master, Let Me Walk with Thee"
found in:
UMH: 430   NCH: 503
H82: 659/660   CH: 602
PH: 357   LBW: 492
NNBH: 445

"Lead Me, Lord"
found in:
UMH: 473   CH: 593
AAHH: 145   Renew: 175
NNBH: 341

"Open My Eyes, that I May See"
found in:
UMH: 454   NNBH: 218
PH: 324   CH: 586

"May You Run and not Be Weary"
found in:
CCB: 99

"God, You Are My God"
found in:
CCB: 60

Prayer for the Day / Collect

O God, who comes to save us, grant us the wisdom to look to you and your reign for our salvation; through Jesus Christ our Savior. Amen.

OR

We come, O God, into your presence to worship and adore you. We are weary from all who have offered us false salvation. Refresh us and guide us once more to your way of truth. Amen.

Prayer of Confession

Leader: Let us confess to God and before one another our sins and especially the way we look for salvation in people and forces other than God.

People: We confess to you, O God, and before one another that we have sinned. We are a foolish people and we are easily led astray. We have heard the promises of politicians and pundits. We have heard sound bites and sales pitches. We have even dared to believe that they were offering us the answer to our problems. How silly we have

been, as we have allowed their banter to draw us from the truth of your way. Only in you is salvation found and only in you will we find the answers. Forgive us and empower us with your Spirit to live into your reign. Amen.
Leader: God knows that we are made of dust and are people of the earth who are fragile and frail. God loves us and welcomes us back to the way of salvation and life.

Prayers of the People (and the Lord's Prayer)
We worship and adore you, O God, because you are the way of truth and the way of salvation. In you alone do we find life abundant and eternal.

(The following paragraph may be used if a separate prayer of confession has not been used.)
We confess to you, O God, and before one another that we have sinned. We are a foolish people, and we are easily led astray. We have heard the promises of politicians and pundits. We have heard sound bites and sales pitches. We have even dared to believe that they were offering us the answer to our problems. How silly we have been, as we have allowed their banter to draw us from the truth of your way. Only in you is salvation found and only in you will we find the answers. Forgive us and empower us with your Spirit to live into your reign.

We give you thanks for all the ways in which you have led us as your people. You walked with us in the garden, through the sea, and in the wilderness. You have always sought to lead us to the Promised Land.

(Other thanksgivings may be offered.)
We offer to your care and love those who have been led astray by hucksters, politicians, false messiahs, and their own hearts. We pray for those we meet each day without recognizing their lostness.

(Other intercessions may be offered.)
All these things we ask in the name of our Savior Jesus Christ, who taught us to pray together, saying:
Our Father... Amen.

(Or if the Lord's Prayer is not used at this point in the service)
All this we ask in the name of the Blessed and Holy Trinity. Amen.

Proper 28
Pentecost 26
Ordinary Time 33

Isaiah 65:17-25
2 Thessalonians 3:6-13
Luke 21:5-19

Call to Worship
Leader: Surely God is our salvation.
People: We will trust and not be afraid.
Leader: God is our strength and our might.
People: God has become our salvation.
Leader: With joy let us draw water from the wells of salvation.
People: Great in our midst is the Holy One of Israel.

OR

Leader: Come, for Jesus calls us.
People: We come because of Christ's gracious invitation.
Leader: Bring others with you to the fount of living waters.
People: We will bring them by hook or by crook.
Leader: Bring them as Jesus brought you.
People: We will love them into the presence of God.

Hymns and Sacred Songs
"Hope of the World"
found in:

UMH: 178	NCH: 46
H82: 472	CH: 538
PH: 360	LBW: 493

"Fairest Lord Jesus"
found in:
UMH: 189   NCH: 44
H82: 383/384   CH: 97
PH: 306   Renew: 166
NNBH: 75

"There's a Spirit in the Air"
found in:
UMH: 192   CH: 257
PH: 433   Renew: 282
NCH: 294

"I Want to Walk as a Child of the Light"
found in:
UMH: 206   Renew: 152
H82: 490

"I Surrender All"
found in:
UMH: 354   NNBH: 198
AAHH: 396

"Pues Si Vivimos" ("When We Are Living")
found in:
UMH: 356   NCH: 499
PH: 400   CH: 536

"Savior, Like a Shepherd Lead Us"
found in:
UMH: 381   NNBH: 54
H82: 708   NCH: 252
PH: 387   CH: 558
AAHH: 424   LBW: 481

"Jesus Calls Us"
found in:
UMH: 398   NCH: 171/172
H82: 549/550   CH: 337
NNBH: 183   LBW: 494

"I Will Call Upon the Lord" *(this fits very well with the Psalm)*
found in:
CCB: 9   Renew: 15

"Your Loving Kindness Is Better than Life"
found in:
CCB: 26

Prayer for the Day / Collect

O God, who gave us Jesus as the perfect example, grant us the grace to trust him enough to imitate his lifestyle of love; through Jesus Christ our Savior. Amen.

OR

We come to worship you, the God who brings us salvation not by forcing us into submission but by wooing us into a relationship. So fill us with your Spirit this day that we may live out of the abundance of your Spirit as our Savior Jesus has done. Amen.

Prayer of Confession

Leader: Let us confess to God and before one another our sins and especially the way we forsake our ideals to convert others to them.

People: We confess to you, O God, and before one another that we have sinned. We have called ourselves by the name of the Son of God, but we have acted like the sons

and daughters of evil. We have been arrogant and proud, and we have tried to bring others to our side more to confirm that we are right than because we believe the way of Jesus is right. Where Jesus loved and invited, we have tried to conquer and defeat others. Instead of drawing others to the Christ, we have pushed them away because we do not act like him. Forgive us and empower us with your Spirit to live fully into the likeness of the Christ so that we may bear his name in truth. Amen.

Leader: God is patient and kind and waits for his children to come home. God welcomes you so that you may welcome others.

Prayers of the People (and the Lord's Prayer)

We worship and adore you, O God, for you are the mighty one, and yet you are gracious and loving toward us, full of gentle kindness.

(The following paragraph may be used if a separate prayer of confession has not been used.)

We confess to you, O God, and before one another that we have sinned. We have called ourselves by the name of the Son of God, but we have acted like the sons and daughters of evil. We have been arrogant and proud, and we have tried to bring others to our side more to confirm that we are right than because we believe the way of Jesus is right. Where Jesus loved and invited, we have tried to conquer and defeat others. Instead of drawing others to the Christ, we have pushed them away because we do not act like him. Forgive us and empower us with your Spirit to live fully into the likeness of the Christ so that we may bear his name in truth.

We give you thanks for all the ways you have tenderly called us to yourself. You have drawn us with bands of love, and you have wooed us to your way of life, eternal and abundant. You have always acted for our good and the good of all your creation.

(Other thanksgivings may be offered.)
We pray for one another in our need and especially for our need to be open to your gentle calling. The forces of evil speak so loudly and powerfully that many are trapped in their lies. We know how persuasive those voices can be at times. As you continue to call your children home, empower us with your loving Spirit, that we may also be part of your call and not part of the shouting of evil.

(Other intercessions may be offered.)
All these things we ask in the name of our Savior Jesus Christ, who taught us to pray together, saying:
Our Father . . . Amen.

(Or if the Lord's Prayer is not used at this point in the service)
All this we ask in the name of the Blessed and Holy Trinity. Amen.

Christ the King
(Proper 29 / Ordinary Time 34)

Jeremiah 23:1-6
Colossians 1:11-20
Luke 23:33-43

Call to Worship
Leader: God has raised up a mighty Savior for us.
People: We have seen the promised mercy of our God.
Leader: We have been rescued from our enemies.
People: Let us therefore serve God with gladness.
Leader: God's light is upon those who sit in darkness.
People: It will guide our feet into the way of peace.

OR

Leader: Come and worship our God and sovereign.
People: We come to worship and adore our God.
Leader: Let us submit ourselves to the reign of God in Christ.
People: We are God's obedient servants.
Leader: Let us live as the people of God.
People: We live to serve God and God's reign.

Hymns and Sacred Songs
"Crown Him with Many Crowns"
found in:

UMH: 327	NCH: 301
H82: 494	CH: 234
PH: 151	LBW: 170
AAHH: 288	Renew: 56
NNBH: 125	

"Hail, Thou Once-Despised Jesus"
found in:
UMH: 325   H82: 495

"Rejoice, the Lord Is King"
found in:
UMH: 715/716   NCH: 303
H82: 481   CH: 699
PH: 155   LBW: 171

"Hail to the Lord's Anointed"
found in:
UMH: 203   CH: 140
H82: 616   LBW: 87
AAHH: 187   Renew: 101
NCH: 104

"All Hail the Power of Jesus' Name"
found in:
UMH: 154/155   NCH: 304
H82: 450/451   CH: 91/92
PH: 142/143   LBW: 328/329
AAHH: 292/294   Renew: 45
NNBH: 315

"Jesus Shall Reign"
found in:
UMH: 157   NCH: 300
H82: 544   CH: 95
PH: 423   LBW: 530
NNBH: 10   Renew: 296

"Alleluia, Alleluia"
found in:
UMH: 162   CH: 40

H82: 178　　　　　　　Renew: 271
PH: 106

"Lift High the Cross"
found in:
UMH: 159　　　　　　NCH: 198
H82: 473　　　　　　　CH: 108
PH: 371　　　　　　　　LBW: 377
AAHH: 242　　　　　　Renew: 297

"All Hail King Jesus"
found in:
CCB: 29　　　　　　　Renew: 35

"Lord, I Lift Your Name on High"
found in:
CCB: 36　　　　　　　Renew: 4

Prayer for the Day / Collect

O God, who is sovereign over all creation, grant to us, your servants, the grace to serve you and your reign with faithfulness and joy in this life and in the life to come; through Jesus Christ our Savior. Amen.

OR

We come to bow before you, O sovereign of all creation, for we are your people and the subjects of your reign. Receive our praise and empower us to live as your faithful people. Amen.

Prayer of Confession

Leader: Let us confess to God and before one another our sins and especially the way we are so quick to assert our rights and so slow to accept our responsibilities.

People: We confess to you, O God, and before one another that we have sinned. We have claimed the name of Christ and thought that gave us special status. We have failed to take on the responsibilities of serving with Christ. We long to see him high and exalted, and we easily forget that he came in the form of a slave to serve you and others. We have not been true citizens of your reign but have tried to shape it to our advantage. Forgive us and empower us with your Spirit, so that we might take our place as faithful members of your Christ. Amen.

Leader: God's reign is open to all and God welcomes the stranger and the straggler into the fold.

Prayers of the People (and the Lord's Prayer)

We worship and adore you, sovereign of all, for it is by your love and grace that we exist. You are the Creator and are the ruler over all that is.

(The following paragraph may be used if a separate prayer of confession has not been used.)

We confess to you, O God, and before one another that we have sinned. We have claimed the name of Christ and thought that gave us special status. We have failed to take on the responsibilities of serving with Christ. We long to see him high and exalted, and we easily forget that he came in the form of a slave to serve you and others. We have not been true citizens of your reign but have tried to shape it to our advantage. Forgive us and empower us with your Spirit, so that we might take our place as faithful members of your Christ.

We give you thanks for all the ways we see your gracious rule at work in our world and in our lives.

(Other thanksgivings may be offered.)

We pray for those who are still seeking a place to belong and a cause to which they can give their lives. We pray for those who have not yet discovered the joy of being your subjects or the lightness of your yoke.

(Other intercessions may be offered.)
All these things we ask in the name of our Savior Jesus Christ, who taught us to pray together, saying:
Our Father... Amen.

(Or if the Lord's Prayer is not used at this point in the service)
All this we ask in the name of the Blessed and Holy Trinity. Amen.

Thanksgiving Day

Deuteronomy 26:1-11
Philippians 4:4-9
John 6:25-35

Call to Worship
Leader: Let the whole world shout for joy to God.
People: We come into God's presence with singing.
Leader: It is God who has made us.
People: We are God's people, God's sheep.
Leader: Give thanks to God and bless God's name.
People: Our God is good, steadfast in love, and faithful forever.

OR

Leader: Come and give thanks to God.
People: We give thanks to our God from whom every good gift comes.
Leader: Come and acknowledge that we are people of need.
People: We come as mere mortals with no claims on God's love.
Leader: Let us rejoice in God's goodness and love for all creation.
People: With joy we share God's love to all.

Hymns and Sacred Songs
"Come, Ye Thankful People, Come"
found in:

UMH: 694	NNBH: 327
H82: 290	NCH: 422
PH: 551	CH: 718
AAHH: 194	LBW: 407

"Now Thank We All Our God"
found in:

UMH: 102
H82: 396/397
PH: 555
NNBH: 330

NCH: 419
CH: 715
LBW: 533/534

"We Gather Together"
found in:

UMH: 131
H82: 433
PH: 559

NNBH: 326
NCH: 421
CH: 276

"All Creatures of Our God and King"
found in:

UMH: 62
H82: 400
PH: 455
AAHH: 147

NNBH: 33
NCH: 17
CH: 22
Renew: 47

"For the Beauty of the Earth"
found in:

UMH: 92
H82: 416
PH: 473
NNBH: 8

NCH: 28
CH: 56
LBW: 561

"Many and Great, O God"
found in:

UMH: 148
H82: 385
PH: 271

NCH: 3
CH: 58

"God of the Sparrow, God of the Whale"
found in:

| UMH: 122 | NCH: 32 |
| PH: 272 | CH: 70 |

"For the Fruits of this Creation"
found in:

UMH: 97	NCH: 425
H82: 424	CH: 714
PH: 553	LBW: 563

"Give Thanks"
found in:

| CCB: 92 | Renew: 266 |

"For the Gift of Creation"
found in:
CCB: 67

Prayer for the Day / Collect
O God, who without consideration of persons gives to all, grant us the grace to acknowledge you as the giver of all good gifts and ourselves as having no claim on your love; through Jesus Christ our Savior. Amen.

OR

We come to worship and adore you, O God, for you are the giver of all good gifts and the lover of the unlovely. You do not wait for us to earn your love but offer it without price to all. Fill us with your Spirit this day that we may go out and imitate your loving actions. Amen.

Prayer of Confession
Leader: Let us confess to God and before one another our sins and especially the way we view ourselves as better and more deserving of your love than others.

People: We confess to you, O God, and before one another that we have sinned. We have received so much from your hand, and yet we act as if we produced it by our own works. We look at others and judge them as less worthy than ourselves. We have forgotten our heritage, which, however glorious in human terms, is but the heritage of creatures and not of Creator. Forgive us our blindness and open our eyes by the power of your Spirit that we might truly be thankful for your goodness and open to sharing it with others. Amen.

Leader: God's good gifts include the gift of forgiveness and the opportunity to amend life. With thanksgiving, live as God's children.

Prayers of the People (and the Lord's Prayer)

We worship and give praise to the God of Creation, who opens the hand and feeds the creature. Your kindness offers to us all that we need for a life that is full of joy and abundance.

(The following paragraph may be used if a separate prayer of confession has not been used.)

We confess to you, O God, and before one another that we have sinned. We have received so much from your hand, and yet we act as if we produced it by our own works. We look at others and judge them as less worthy than ourselves. We have forgotten our heritage, which, however glorious in human terms, is but the heritage of creatures and not of Creator. Forgive us our blindness and open our eyes by the power of your Spirit that we might truly be thankful for your goodness and open to sharing it with others.

We thank you for all the good gifts we have received from your hand. You have given us a wonderful world filled with all we need to survive and to live abundantly with joy.

Most of all we thank you for Jesus, who has shown us how to live with joy and thanksgiving always.

(Other thanksgivings may be offered.)
We offer to your care and help those who find it hard to be thankful at this time of year. There are those who are sick and dying, those who are grieving, those who do not have the things they need to sustain their lives or the lives of their loved ones. There are those who are oppressed by governments, addictions, and family members. As you seek them out and offer them your love and life, help us to be messengers of your love to all we come in contact with this week.

(Other intercessions may be offered.)
All these things we ask in the name of our Savior Jesus Christ, who taught us to pray together, saying:
Our Father... Amen.

(Or if the Lord's Prayer is not used at this point in the service)
All this we ask in the name of the Blessed and Holy Trinity. Amen.

If You Like This Book...

George Reed has also written **Lectionary Worship Aids**, Series IX, Cycle B (978-0-7880-2669-0) (printed book $29.95, e-book $19.95) and Reed contributed Pentecost (first third) "Living in the Spirit" to **Sermons on the Gospel Readings**, Series II, Cycle B (978-0-7880-2370-5) (printed book $36.95, e-book $24.95).

Other Lectionary Worship Aids titles

Lectionary Worship Aids, Series VIII, Cycle A
Thom Shuman
978-0-7880-2456-6
printed book $18.95 / e-book $9.95

Lectionary Worship Aids, Series VII, Cycle A
Frank Ramirez
978-0-7880-2317-0
printed book $23.95 / e-book $9.95

Series VII, Cycle B
978-0-7880-2363-7
printed book $21.95 / e-book $9.95

Series VII, Cycle C
978-0-7880-2404-7
printed book $24.95 / e-book $19.95

For other Lectionary Worship Aids resources, please visit www.csspub.com and type "lectionary worship aids" in the Search box option on the left hand side of the page.

contact CSS Publishing Company, Inc.
www.csspub.com   **800-241-4056**

Prices are subject to change without notice.